Backyard Chickens A Practical Handbook to Raising Chickens

CLAIRE WOODS

CONTENTS

1 STARTING OUT
THE JOYS OF CHICKENS

In todays' stressful world, it can be hard to find time to relax and escape from work – unless you have chickens! There is something peaceful, relaxing and amusing about watching these barnyard birds go about their business. They talk amongst themselves and always greet you like you haven't been home for days - they require little but give so much in return.

There are people out there with anxieties, and children with ADHD who have had their lives and abilities improved by keeping chickens. It may sound daft, but in relating to the birds they become more relaxed and focused.

There is also the knowledge that your birds are giving you fresh eggs on a daily basis. Right now there is a huge emphasis on making poultry farms more humane in the treatment of their birds. What can be more natural than watching your own flock wandering peacefully around the yard?

We also read about salmonella contamination of meat and eggs from the agricultural and food industry on a regular basis. As the 'farmer' you are sure of where your eggs or meat have come from and the chances are your birds are a lot cleaner and better cared for than factory hens.

Many people worry about what has been 'added' to the supermarket chicken. If you raise your own birds you will know exactly what they have been eating. Although growth hormones were stopped in chickens a few years back, low dose antibiotics are still given to many industrial flocks.

Chickens are great at pest control too! If you let those ladies loose in your garden, the bug population will decrease within a short period of time. Once the gardening year is over you can simply let the girls loose and they will happily scratch away and turn the top soil over for you.

How Much Space Do They Need?

If your hens are going to remain in a coop and run area on a permanent basis, each hen has a square foot requirement.

Heavy birds (Orpington, Rhode Island Red, Delaware, and Easter Egger etc.) will require four square feet of coop and ten square feet of run per bird. Since heavy birds rarely fly, the space accommodation needs to be ground level or slightly higher. Perches at two to three feet off the ground can offer extra square footage.

Light and/or bantam birds (Barbu D'Uccle, Serama etc.) will require two square feet of coop and eight square feet of run per bird. If you have bantam birds, it's easy to accommodate the space requirements by building vertically since they love to fly short distances and can get up higher than heavier birds.

It is also recommended that you allow one square foot of roosting space per bird.

Although they may spread out during the summer heat, in winter you will find all your hens crammed together in a group at one end of the perch! They save energy and stay warm by doing this and manage to tolerate each other pretty well for the sake of staying warm.

Of course you can cram more birds into the space, but this will usually lead to anti-social behaviors such as picking. While less coop room may be fine in the summer months, in winter chickens can suffer from boredom– then the trouble begins. Feather picking, vent picking and toe picking are all boredom related bad behaviors and can have a severe health impact on the lower order hens.

If your space for the hens is tight, you will need to be inventive about keeping them occupied. Toys, treat dispensers and mirrors are all diversions which the hens seem to enjoy. Place perches at different heights so they can practice their aerobics and escape from the bullies. Repurposing an old wooden ladder cut to size provides several perches at different heights.

If they are going to be under 'supervised free range' for part of the day, the requirement will be slightly less. If they are free range/pastured all day you can get away with less room in the coop since they will only spend time there to lay an egg and sleep.

Always bear in mind that winter is a time when they are all together in the space you have provided. Depending on where you live, winter can be long and it's likely that they won't want to be out foraging in the cold and snow. This means they will be inside looking for mischief! Make sure you have plenty of things to keep them occupied and enough space that there is room for all. If you can provide an area for them to dust bathe in they will love you forever and it will keep parasites down to a minimum.

Typical Time Commitment

This can vary with the size of your flock. If you have six hens, your daily time commitment need be no more than fifteen minutes in the morning and fifteen minutes in the evening. This is 'bare minimum' time.

The more time you spend with your birds, the tamer they will become. It really will pay off in the long run to have the girls be comfortable in your presence. At any given time you may need to do health checks, administer medication or even take a bird to the veterinarian - it is much easier to do if your hen is comfortable with being picked up and held.

Of course, with larger flocks the time commitment will be more, so be prepared to adjust your schedule as needed. It will also depend on what you wish to do with your birds – eggs, meat, raising chicks or specialized breeding. The more complex your needs the more time you will need to invest in your flock.

Before you invest in chickens and chicken paraphernalia, think hard about what your intent is. Do you simply want eggs, meat or both? Do you want to breed a certain variety? Knowing your goal beforehand will save you a lot of time and money.

Basic Chicken Behavior

Communication

Chickens can and do communicate very well within the flock and with you if you pay attention! Studies of chicken behaviors over the years indicate that chicken have over thirty different vocalizations, many with specific meanings regarding mating, nesting, hierarchy, danger and distress. They also use their other senses such as sight, smell and touch to convey more subtle signals to each other.

There are different calls for 'I've laid an egg', 'danger!' and 'come quick' to name just three. It has been discovered that chickens have a different call for ground danger (snake etc.) and sky danger (hawk). They can and do look out for flock safety. Momma hen communicates with her chicks while they are still in the egg, so bonding with them before they hatch. The unhatched embryo also communicates with its' unborn siblings forming strong bonds prior to hatching.

When you hear them lying in the sun murmuring contentedly they are maintaining communication with each other, much like human chit-chat around the pool. They are ensuring that they can hear one another in case of danger.

Chickens can learn the solutions to some quite sophisticated problems and they can also be deceptive and cunning. Scientists have found some of their cognitive abilities to be on a par with a human toddler. They are intelligent and quite advanced in the realm of understanding and solving some complex problems.

Table Manners

The social structure of a flock is called 'the pecking order'. A new addition to the flock will quickly learn their place in the hierarchy- the bottom rung of the ladder. Many birds are quick learners and social climbers, they will work their way up the ladder pretty quickly. A docile bird will likely stay on the lowest level until a new bird arrives.

In this organized structure, top birds get to eat first, breed first and 'rule the roost' until they are challenged and beaten by a younger bird. The behavior that they exhibit is very similar to their distant forebears- the wild jungle fowl. It truly is survival of the fittest.

Sleeping

Chickens 'go to roost' each night. This simply means they find a safe perch with others, tuck their heads under their wings and sleep. On closer inspection though, we find that that chickens do not sleep quite like mammals. Although they do experience REM (rapid eye movement) it only occurs for a few seconds at a time, so hens do dream! They also have 'slow wave' sleep similar to humans. During this phase, the day's memories and information are assimilated and stored for future use.

Chickens have the unique ability to experience what is called unihemispheric slow wave sleep. This means that chickens can sleep with one eye open while the opposite side of the brain sleeps. The birds on either end of the roosting bar sleep with the outer eye open and the inner eye shut- they are the lookouts for danger. They usually turn around at some point and let the other eye/brain rest and maintain watch with the opposite side. It has been noted that the birds in the middle will sleep with both eyes shut. Those in the middle are usually higher in the 'pecking order' than those at the ends.

So, if you see your hen with one eye shut and one open she is awake, but also asleep!

Socializing

Chickens are very social birds, after all they usually flock together, but this flock behavior is also a survival tactic. If one bird utters a warning call all will either freeze in position or run for cover. The slowest will become the victim of the predator.

Chicken social arrangements are not all about survival though. Their hierarchy is quite complex with each bird having a specific status in relation to each other. They are able to recognize around one hundred flock mates and know that bird's status in the flock. They also self-compare against other birds in the flock. The 'top' birds are the leaders from whom everyone else learns. There is a very sophisticated order to group activities such as foraging with each bird knowing its' role in the group.

Chickens will also form loose attachments to other species such as humans, cats and dogs.

Mating

Mating and courtship is much more involved than you might think. Roosters will try to entice females with 'tidbitting'- finding a tasty morsel for the hen to eat. He will 'cluck- cluck' excitedly to call her over and inspect his offering. A hen will actually evaluate each potential suitor in his abilities such as food finding, plumage and behavior.

Subordinate males will use strategies of cunning and deception to lure females away from the head rooster in an attempt to mate. Often, this strategy does pay off and the lower rooster gets to mate sporadically.

The mating itself can be very rough for a favorite hen. The rooster hops on her back, grabbing her head or neck feathers and 'treading' her back during the event. This can lead to some favorite hens' having very ragged feathers or bald spots. If a rooster is overly zealous, he should be removed before he really damages a hen.

Scratching

Scratching is a common behavior for chickens. In the wild, jungle fowl will spend about sixty percent of their time scratching and foraging. While our modern hens spend considerably less time doing this, some breeds are fabulous foragers gaining much of their nutrition from the garden and ground. Hens scratch the ground in search of insects, seeds, worms, small pieces of grit and other nutritious goodies such as weeds and grasses. Chickens seem to have an inbuilt knowledge of what their bodies need, so providing them with grass and dirt to scratch in helps them to complete their nutrition.

Dust Bathing

Dust bathing is extremely important for chickens. It helps them to keep their bodies clean. The slight abrasiveness of dirt removes dead skin and parasites from the feathers. The dirt is also cooling to the body on very hot days. Hens cannot sweat, so they use measures such as panting and dust bathing to keep cool.

If your chickens are totally confined, it would be in their best interests if you could supply them with a dust bath. It really doesn't have to be huge. An area the size of a cat litter box would be sufficient for a few hens, but as with many things bigger would be better! In watching hens dust bathing, several will indulge at the same time, all chattering away to each other. It's a strangely peaceful and pleasant sight. After the bath comes the preening. Chickens have an oil gland at the base of their tail. They squeeze this gland to extract oil which they deposit all over the feathers to keep them looking sleek and shiny. The oiling also helps to protect the feathers from damage from the weather or harsh climate conditions.

If you don't provide them with a dust bath area and you allow them to free range, they will create their own. They will excavate shallow depressions in the ground and use it as a bath. One particular area of my garden looks like the surface of the moon! Some of the craters are really deep enough for the unsuspecting person to turn an ankle.

Chapter 1 Checklist

- Know how much space chickens need
- Calculate how much space your flock will need
- Understand the basics of chicken behavior (eg. pecking order and dust bathes).

2 CHOOSING THE CORRECT BREED

Several hundred years ago, man discovered that wild jungle fowl was good to eat and on further investigation, he found the eggs were good too. At some point he started to domesticate them as a portable food source for his family. When humans started to settle down in towns and villages, people started to try and refine the chickens they had. Strangely enough, chickens weren't really appreciated as a barnyard animal until the turn of the last century.

The Victorians were fascinated by the humble chicken and began to cross breed with the intent of creating a 'better bird'; even Queen Victoria had chickens! Of course, the Japanese had been breeding the gorgeous Onagadori fowl for its stunning plumage for many years before the Victorians became interested in breeding chickens.

Here we are in the twenty first century with a stunning array of chickens to choose from. How many different breeds are there? Truthfully, no-one really knows, but it is estimated to be in the hundreds. There are birds that have been specifically bred for enhanced egg laying, quality meat, fighting and plumage.

Let's now look at the different chicken breeds and their purposes to help you choose the best breed for your needs.

Heritage or Production: What's the Difference?

Heritage Breeds
The Livestock Conservancy defines a Heritage chicken as a

natural breeding chicken that has a slow growth rate and can live a long, productive outdoor life. The breed must also conform to the American Poultry Associations standard for that breed. Well known examples of these breeds would be Delaware, Rhode Island and Wyandottes.

Figure 1: A Golden Laced Wyandotte

There are also 'landrace' birds. These are domesticated chickens that have adapted to the land around them. They have been subject to 'natural selection' and the birds are hardy and self-sufficient. Two good examples would be the Icelandic Chicken and the Swedish Flower Hen. Both these breeds have been relatively isolated from other breeds and both are making a comeback in recent years. These birds can be put under the 'heritage' heading, but do not conform to APA standards.

Production Breeds

Production breeds are bred for fast growth rate in meat birds or exceptional egg laying. The life expectancy for production birds is usually much shorter than heritage breeds. The urge to go broody (don't worry if you don't know what broody means we will discuss it later on in the book!) has been virtually eliminated from these birds. Finally, they do not conform to APA standards.

Egg Layers

These hens have been bred to produce large quantities of eggs through their short production lifetimes. Leghorns are a good example of prolific egg producers as are Australorps. There are several types of sex link chickens and they are 'production' egg layers. What is sex link? The phrase simply means that when the chicks hatch, it is possible to discern the males from the females at day one.

Figure 2: A Leghorn Chicken

Meat birds (also known as Broilers)

These birds grow very, very quickly. They put on weight at an alarming rate and are ready for slaughter at around nine weeks. Should they be spared, they will soon die from heart problems. Once they have reached the desired size and weight, it is almost impossible for them to move around since their legs will not hold them up. They have been crossbred and refined over the years to produce a bird that will be economical to feed and quickly be 'table ready'. Examples of these birds would be: Cornish Rock Hens, Red Rangers and Jersey Giants.

Dual Purpose

These hens are the best of both worlds in utility terms. They are productive in the egg department and also grow large enough to be used as a meat bird later on in their life. They also tend to produce eggs for longer than the pure egg laying breeds, although not as many eggs.

If you want a hen that produces a good amount of eggs per week and can be eventually used for meat, the dual purpose hen is for you. A dual purpose hen usually retains some instinct to 'go broody', so it is possible to raise your own chicks (assuming you have a rooster). If you intend to continue keeping chickens, it is economical (and fun) to raise your own chicks.

Common Breeds for Backyard Enthusiasts

The average homesteader is not usually interested in fancy, flighty or high maintenance breeds. The large majority of people that keep chickens in their yard do so for eggs, meat or both. Calm and steady breeds are the order of the day in most cases. If you have children doing a 4H project, you need co-operative and docile hens.

Many people have mixed flocks; this means they have more than one breed of bird in their flock. There really is no right or wrong in having flocks that are mixed or single breed, it is based on what you prefer. Each bird has its own particular 'niche' in the world of poultry. As an example, lots of folks like Silkies because they look different and are cute to look at. While they don't lay that many eggs, they will in general sit on and incubate any eggs you care to give them. So if you want to hatch eggs of a particular breed, give them to the Silkie, it is said they could hatch a rock!

Below you will find a list of breeds that are most suitable for beginner chicken keepers in the US. We have divided them into categories of dual purpose, meat and egg laying breeds.

Egg Laying Breeds

Leghorns are a good layer of white eggs who is also friendly and a good forager. Sex Link Birds are an exceptionally good egg layer with an unfortunately short production life (two-three years). Hamburgs are a good layer of white eggs known for its docile temperament and medium sized eggs. New Hampshire are a great layer of light brown eggs. Has a pea comb making it very cold hardy, but can be a noisy breed. Faverolles are a good layer of creamy/white eggs but is known for being a loud breed. Ideal for a cold climate.

Meat Breeds

Cornish rock cross are a crossbred breed that is the most popular breed for meat- this is your 'supermarket' hen. Jersey Giant are a heritage breed which grows slowly so cannot be rushed to the table. They are incredibly hardy and docile.

Dual Purpose Breeds

Rhode Island Reds are a calm, curious and vocal chicken who is a good layer of brown eggs. This breed is also cold hardy. Bresse are an old breed originally from France which is becoming popular again. Their meat is said to be excellent and they are a good layer also. Delaware is an American breed, which is well known for being friendly and cold hardy. Dorking is an ancient breed from England, seeing new popularity again and renowned for its gentle nature. Australorp are a calm good natured chicken who is tolerant of both hot and cold climates. Sussex is a breed which comes in several different strains including speckled and light. It's a very popular choice for 4H projects. Orpington are a large calm bird which lays well but is known for going broody.

Chapter 2 Checklist

• Understand the difference between egg laying, meat and dual purpose chickens
• Choose your preferred breed of chicken.

3 PLANNING AND BUYING YOUR CHICKENS

It's time to take the plunge! You want chickens and know which breed you'd like but aren't sure where to start. This chapter will help you to plan and choose your starter flock. We start by discussing the various ages you can buy hens at, before moving onto the specifics of where to buy them and also how to transport them properly.

What Should I Start With?

When you get chickens for the first time you have a few different choices. We are going to look at the good and bad of each option. You can buy hatching eggs, day old chicks, started pullets or adult birds. Each choice has its merits but it's really about what you feel is best for you and fits into your schedule well.

Hatching Eggs

Hatching eggs can be bought from online sellers or locally if you have a breeder nearby. They are usually sold by the half dozen or dozen and many sellers will also put a couple of extra eggs in just in case of breakage.

Locally obtained eggs usually hatch the best. Eggs really don't travel well and expected hatch rates can be as low as fifty percent from 'postal' hatching eggs. Of course, you need to have an incubator on hand and know how to work it. If you are brand new to chickens, I really don't recommend that you get hatching eggs unless you really know what you are doing. Although incubation is fairly straightforward, there definitely is an art to it.

People who are looking to breed rare or exotic fowl use incubators a lot since the eggs are far more affordable than pullets or hens. You also need to bear in mind the eggs cannot be sexed, so it is possible that you will end up with roosters. This would not be a good thing if you are in a 'no roosters' zone.

Day Old Chicks

This is the most used and wise choice for novices. You can select which breed(s) you want and when you want them. You can buy sexed chickens thus eliminating non-productive roosters and with many hatcheries you can buy as few as six hens, all different breeds.

When the chicks are delivered by the Postal service, you should open the box in front of the carrier. If there are dead chicks you will need to call the company and start any necessary paperwork for the Postal service and the seller. A word of caution here, sometimes chicks don't survive the journey, so don't have the kids help you open the box unless you are ok with that.

There is a moral dilemma attached to ordering like this though. All male chicks are killed at birth because they are not as 'valuable' as female chicks. Many people feel that this is not acceptable and won't order from these companies.

Chicks

In feed stores and farm stores you will find bins of day old chicks for sale. By the time you buy them they will be older than a day, but that's really not an issue. Occasionally, you will find sexed chicks but more often than not they will be 'straight run' (this means the chicks will be unsexed so you could be buying either hens or roosters).

You will also find that the selection of breeds is limited, but they are usually great for first timers and include: Barred Rocks, Sussex, Rhode Island Reds and Sex Links.

A concern with buying from the farm stores is that these chicks have now been exposed to all sorts of germs. They look healthy now but will they stay that way? A question that you might find is difficult for staff to answer is: are they vaccinated against any chicken ailments such as Mareks?

If you decide to buy this way, make sure they are vaccinated and that you choose the liveliest chicks in the bin, the quiet ones may be sick or weak which is something you don't want in your flock.

Started Pullets

Pullets are birds aged between four months to six months. The chicks have been reared to adulthood and are usually sold at point of lay, meaning the pullet is about to lay her first egg anytime soon! You should also be aware that changes in the bird's routines or surroundings may push back the first egg by a few weeks.

It will depend on whether or not they have been hand reared as to the overall friendliness of the birds. Hand reared birds are the most friendly you can get and are usually calm around people and easily adjust to changes around them. Pullets that have not been hand reared can become friendly with you; it just takes a bit more time and effort.

Adult Birds

Adult hens are more difficult to come by as breeders like to move birds out before they get too old since they eat more. If you find some adults don't forget to ask how old they are; chickens over the age of three won't lay many eggs. The majority of chickens are highly productive for the first couple of years then their egg laying slows down.

A common source of adult hens is animal shelters or rescue sanctuaries. Frequently people buy chicks with enthusiasm, but then interest wanes and the hens become neglected. There are several shelters dedicated to rescuing birds and will re-home them for a small fee. If you do get some of these birds you should know that they will be unlikely to give you many eggs for some time if at all. Ex-battery hens are usually completely depleted of energy by the time they are 'let go'. It will take several months of intensive care and attention to get them back to being a normal chicken. In terms of reward, watching an ex-battery enjoy the sun, grass and all things chicken is probably the greatest reward you could wish for.

In financial terms, the cheapest option is the chicks. Pullets will cost you more because of the care, feed and time expended to raise the bird. Adult hens in their prime are the most expensive. Rescue and ex-battery hens are usually cheaper than pullets but more expensive than chicks.

Choosing the Sex

Choosing the sex of your birds is usually a no brainer. If you want eggs or meat then hens will do the job. However, if you wish to breed your birds for your own pleasure or profit, you will certainly need a rooster!

Roosters get a bad rap in general. Humans are usually guilty of wanting to be able to hold and cuddle with their birds, but this is not what your rooster is about. Although some roosters love to be held and petted, roosters in general take their job very seriously. Their task in life is to protect the hens against predators (this includes you if you are seen as a threat). This makes him appear totally indifferent to you and your bribes, he's not being unfriendly it's just that his brain is wired this way.

Tip: There are some very mean roosters out there and they will pass their attitudes to the male chicks, so they should not be mated...unless you want mean roosters.

How Many Chicks Should I Get?

You can generally average out how many chicks you will need. If your birds are for eggs only, then you just need to think how many eggs do you use in a week currently? One hen will average four to five eggs a week. Throw in a couple of extra chicks for 'just in case' and you have your number!

For example if you want 16 eggs a week you would need 6 hens (4 would normally do this many eggs but I've included 2 'just in case' chicks).

If you want to sell your eggs you need to sit down and think about where you are going to market them. Will they be for friends and family only? If you want to do it commercially you will have to dive into the legal requirements of your locale which can involve inspection of your premises and permits.

Where Do I Get My Chicks?

The best place for beginners to buy their chickens from is a local farmer, hatchery or farm supply stores. Though, if you want to purchase your chickens from further away the USPS has been shipping chicks for about one hundred years and will ship chicks which you purchase online.

Hatcheries

Ordering your chicks online is quick and simple... once you know which breeds you want! Most large hatcheries allow quantities as small as six to be shipped to you. The chicks can be mixed breeds if you wish. Possibly the biggest benefit is that you can have sexed chicks, which eliminates the chance of getting a rooster. However, you should know that even professional chicken sexers (yes, there is such a job), are only right about ninety percent of the time, so be prepared to take back the occasional rooster.

Feed Stores

Farm and feed stores usually sell unsexed chicks, so you have a fifty-fifty chance of getting at least one rooster! The selection of breeds is usually limited to the more popular backyard breeds, so if you want something a bit different, for example a Silkie, you will have to look to the internet or local breeders. Sometimes if your order is large enough the feed store will order these rarer breeds online for you, however it is cheaper to do it yourself online.

Private Breeders

If you are buying from a private breeder you really need to do some checking first. Try to ask around in your local area to find out what their reputation is like. There are literally hundreds if not thousands of people who call themselves 'breeders'. Chickens are big business and there is money to be made, so be sure to check them out. Reputable breeders are a cut above and subsequently your chicks may cost you a little more, but it will definitely be worth it in the long run.

Shows and Festivals

Folks who participate in poultry shows and exhibit at festivals and fairs are usually very proud of their birds. They spend a lot of time and money in making sure the birds are in first class condition. Although you may not be able to purchase the award winning bird itself, the owner will likely sell you some of the other birds they have. The birds in these shows are usually NPIP approved (National Poultry Improvement Program) and will have been tested for disease. Please note these birds will not be cheap though and I wouldn't recommend them for beginners.

Auctions

If you are new to the world of poultry, it must be stressed that auctions are not the place to buy good quality stock in general. Local livestock auctions can range from good to extremely bad. Livestock is often sold and re-sold several times which stresses the bird tremendously as they are subjected to all sorts of possible infections. I would avoid auctions unless you have an expert to take with you.

Local 'Chicken Lady

You may be lucky enough to have a neighbor who is selling chickens or chicks. Make sure you can inspect the bird and their living conditions before you commit. The vast majority of backyard chicken keepers are good people who treat their animals well, but there are exceptions. If you don't like the look of the birds don't be afraid to say no and walk away.

Poultry Clubs

If you have access to a local poultry club or groups then use it! These folks have been around chickens longer than you so they have a wealth of information to share with you. You will soon find that 'chicken people' love to talk about their birds! They of course can point you in the right direction for buying birds and perhaps will sell you some of their own.

What Should I Look Out For?

All birds should have clear, bright eyes. They should be curious about their environment and you. Feathers or fluff should look clean with good coloring.

Make sure to take a look at the feet; are there any splayed toes or deformities? A bird should hold itself upright and be alert to its surroundings. In feathered birds check carefully for lice or other parasites, check the vent area too (it should be clean and moist). In a pullet, the vent will be a very pale pinkish/white until she starts to lay and as she lays it will then become a deeper pink. In older birds, if the vent area is pale pink/white, she has likely gone past her laying years.

If a bird, regardless of age, exhibits any of these signs you should avoid buying it:

- Sleepy, lethargic
- Hunched into a ball
- Sitting by itself
- Reluctant to move
- Any nasal/eye discharge
- Blocked vent

Note: I hear you asking "what's a blocked vent?" Good question, it applies to chicks only. When a baby chick poops, the poop sometimes gets hard and crusts around their vent effectively sealing the hole shut. The chick will die if the vent is not cleared.

Transporting Your Birds

You can transport your birds in a sturdy cardboard box of appropriate size for the bird: a shoebox will comfortably fit eight chicks for a short journey, whereas a large cardboard box will be need for pullets or adult hens.

If you are transporting them long distances (over 30 minutes) you will need a sturdier container such as a pet carrier, wire cage or plastic tote. If you happen to be driving a substantial distance where you may need to stop for a break, make sure you have cool water available for your birds. It is sensible to give them a 'water break' about every six to eight hours. Remove the water when you are travelling as it will slosh all over the place making the birds wet and miserable. If you have children travelling with you it's smart to not allow them to open the box in the car. Chicks are fast and they can get into very small spaces, if they escape you will be lucky to get them back.

If you are going to be travelling frequently with several birds, you could invest in a plastic carry crate from a poultry supplier. The crate has many air holes, can hold several birds easily and is a dream to clean out.

Chapter 3 Checklist

- Decide what age chickens to buy (e.g. chicks, pullets or adults)
- Plan the size of your flock and remember chicken math!
- You should also know what a healthy chicken looks like

4 HOUSING YOUR FLOCK

Chickens are not very demanding when it comes to houses. They don't need running water, electricity or carpets. A modified basic wooden box will do in a pinch, but there are a few crucial things you need for your flock to ensure their safety and wellbeing. In this chapter we talk through the key requirements of your coop and how to house your flock safely.

Shelter Requirements

This is the most basic need of all, a place where they are able to get out of the blistering sun, howling wind or blowing snow. The coop needs to be water resistant as there is nothing more miserable than a wet chicken. If your coop is outside, you need to check the joints and roof to ensure they are water tight. A drafty coop is not acceptable, as in the winter drafts can cause frostbite on combs, wattles and feet. In addition to being water resistant the coop needs to have ventilation that allows stale, humid air to escape but brings in cool, fresh air too. The vents must be placed correctly to ensure that the draft doesn't blow onto the chickens.

A lot of people ask if the coop has to be insulated for cold winters, and the answer depends much upon where you live. Unless you live in remote parts of Canada or Alaska far up north then your chickens will be fine without insulation. If you decide to insulate the coop, the most common choice is Styrofoam. However, chickens love to peck at this so be sure they cannot access it. If you want to insulate, but can't afford proper insulation, you can get creative. Placing two or three pieces of cardboard on the floor of the nest box will give some warmth, or you can stack straw bales around the outside of the coop.

Tip: Don't stack straw bales inside the coop, you are inviting mold issues.

Truthfully though, chickens are very hardy creatures. Some of our Canadian friends have shared pictures of coops almost buried in the snow with no insulation and their hens are fine. One chicken gives off the equivalent heat of a ten watt light bulb, so ten chickens give off quite a bit of warmth.

To see how cold it gets inside the coop, you can place a thermometer in the center of the room. It will likely read somewhere between thirty two and forty two Fahrenheit when you open up in the morning. If the weather turns exceptionally cold and the hens seem to be suffering you can place an oil fired radiator in the coop on the lowest setting

Tip: Don't use heat lamps or unguarded light bulbs in the coop; fire is an ever present hazard and one that is sadly repeated every year in the form of coop/barn/house fires.

Temperature Controls

Ideally, the coop should be cool in summer and warm in winter.

Correct ventilation of your coop is of paramount importance when it comes to temperature regulation. A good flow of air will keep the coop at an optimal temperature for your hens. If you think it's too hot you need to add more ventilation holes. If you have a large walk-in coop, you can increase the breeze by opening the main door and the 'pop' door. If it is too cold in winter you likely need to adjust your vents to retain some of the warmer air in the coop, also check for any drafts.

Space for Your Hens

Adequate space for birds to co-habit peacefully is essential. If they are crowded in together they are likely to start anti-social behaviors like picking and pecking each other. The worst time for these behaviors is winter; hens get bored and create mischief.

Bantam breeds need less space than larger birds. They will need two square feet of coop space each and eight square feet of run per bird. Large breeds need four square feet of coop space and ten square feet of run space. It's also recommended that each bird have one square foot of roosting space, although they all usually hang together at one end.

If your flock is pastured during the day, the square footage in the coop can be slightly less since they will only be sleeping in the coop. Winter time poses the biggest problem as already noted. They need enough room to be able to have a personal area that is their own inside the coop. You should be able to provide quiet areas for the more timid flock members should they want to hide out or be alone.

Nesting Boxes

With nesting boxes you will need approximately one box for every three hens, but it never hurts to have more. There is always one favorite box that they will squabble over, so more is better. You can use old grape crates, five gallon pails, cardboard boxes or simply buy your nest boxes. The box should be able to accommodate your hen, but not big enough for two to occupy. The average size is about twelve inches by twelve inches and will accommodate most hens perfectly. To increase the available floor space, nest boxes are often built sticking out from the coop.

Roosts

Roosts are simply the place where the birds congregate to sleep at night. They will all generally sleep on the same perch (roost), although some do prefer to be by themselves if they feel perfectly safe. As previously discussed, each hen needs one foot of perch space. They may use this much room in summer when it's hot, but in winter you will find them all huddled together to keep warm.

Fresh Air

Hens should never be kept solely in a coop unless it's an emergency. They enjoy being out and about scratching around and even more importantly, getting fresh air. The air in a coop becomes stale, dusty and can smell of ammonia if not kept clean. Dust and ammonia can irritate the respiratory system of the hen leading to health problems. The coop should be 'aired out' daily to ensure good quality air circulation.

Protection from Predators

Perhaps the most important task of your coop is to stop predators getting access to your flock. Predators come in all shapes and sizes, but they all enjoy a good chicken dinner. Security is of the upmost importance if you want to keep your flock safe. The coop itself needs to be secure as does the run area. This is the perfect place to mention the difference between chicken wire and hardware cloth. Chicken wire will keep chickens contained; however it will not keep predators out. Hardware cloth will keep predators out and chickens in. If you think that the cost of hardware cloth is prohibitive, try thinking about how much it will cost to replace your flock.

Tip: If you can't afford to put in hardware cloth all through the run, at least take it to a height of three feet. This will prevent raccoons from reaching through and grabbing your hens.

If hawks or owls are a problem you can cover the top of the run with chicken wire (it's ok to use it here), or take a ball of strong twine and run in a zig-zag random pattern over the top of the run. This will disrupt the flight path of the larger birds.

Many predators will try and dig their way in: foxes, coyotes, dogs and weasels are all diggers. The best way to prevent this is to dig a trench around the perimeter of the run to a depth of six inches. Bend the hardware cloth into an 'L' shape six inches for each 'arm'. Attach one arm to the base of the run area and bury the wire. This will deter digging by all but the most determined predator. If you live in a city and think you don't have predators around, you are mistaken. Foxes, raccoons, rats and coyotes have all made the city their home and they are thriving.

Coop Security

We have talked about securing the run, so now let's turn our attention to the coop itself. All doors should have tamper-proof locks. You'd be surprised but Raccoons can figure out how to open many types of lock. A lock that requires opposing thumbs to open, such as a 'snap' lock or padlock will keep the predators out. Also it has been known that exotic hens have been stolen by humans so make sure to use a padlock to keep your hens safe.

All vents should be covered with hardware cloth to prevent entry. You should check your coop floors periodically to make sure there aren't any holes that need fixing. Rats and mice will chew their way into your coop to access the food in addition to eggs and small chicks. If you find any holes you need to repair them; a piece of hardware cloth over the hole will do the job. Don't forget to check the roof too, predators are cunning and will spend a lot of time checking out your coop security for weaknesses.

Ranging your Hens

When it comes to raising chickens there are a few types of ranging for your flock, from completely free range (pastured) to completely confined. The best option for you will depend on your location, your reason for keeping chickens, comfort level and available space. Let's take a look at each option in turn.

Free Range

Free range is allowing your flock the freedom to roam over your land. The area can be large or small, but there are no barriers to their wanderings. Perhaps the only fencing would be around your property to mark boundary lines with your neighbors. Whilst this appears 'idyllic' it can become problematic in practice due to predators.

Fenced Range

In a fenced range they are allowed to freely roam within a specified area. The fence serves two purposes: to keep chickens in and secondly, to deter ground predators. This is personally my favorite approach as I can leave my hens during the day knowing that they can't get up to too much trouble! The only notable downside to this approach is if you have a small garden you probably don't want to fence a large section of it off just for your hens.

Chicken Tractors/Portable Shelters

Chicken tractors are lightweight portable shelters that can be moved daily to different areas of your garden. This means they get access to fresh grass and different areas of your garden which stops them from overgrazing any one particular section of your garden. The beauty of these is that they can be and they are quite secure for your flock and come in many shapes and sizes. These are ideal when you don't have a large garden or don't want to put up a permanent fence in your garden.

Build or Buy A Coop?

Building a coop is fairly simple if you have a basic understanding of carpentry and a good skill set. It will not cost anywhere near as much as a ready-made kit. Not only that, it can be fun too. The merits of building your own coop are that you can build to the size you require, save lots of money and you can create something that you want and will suit your hens. One word of caution here: if you have four hens, then build for a dozen, chickens are addictive.

If you decide to go with a pre-made coop then be sure to check the following points:

• Is the wood treated? You don't want your hens pecking at treated wood. The roof however would need to be treated to be waterproof.

• How sturdy is it? A cheap coop is cheap for a reason. Several people have had problems with bought coops splitting, warping and rotting within a year.

• Coop manufacturers are optimistic about how many hens a coop can accommodate. Remember your square footage needs.

• Does the coop come with a useable lock? Would it stand up to a determined fox or raccoon trying to get in?

• Is the coop waterproofed? If not you will have to do this yourself.

• Does it come with a run? If not, can you build onto the coop or will you pasture your flock?

• How is ease of access for you, remember you will need access to clean it.

If you want to build your own chicken coop make sure you check out our other publication on Amazon How to Build Your Own Chicken Coop Guide.

What is a Normal Set Up?

A coop that measures six by six feet would give you thirty six square feet of floor space, which would mean you could house eight large breed hens or eighteen bantams comfortably. You should allow one nest box for every three hens, so three boxes for the larger birds or six boxes for the bantams. The attached run will need to be at least eighty square foot for large breed or one hundred forty four for bantams. Remember with bantams you can build up too, they love to stretch their wings and fly. The run also needs a variety of perches for the flock so they can sit up off the ground, a dust bath area for them and other items to keep them occupied. Bored birds get into mischief, so keep them busy. The run itself should have some sort of covering over a small section of it; this will provide shade during hot weather and ease the snow burden in winter.

Chapter 4 Checklist

• Know what chickens need from their shelter
• Fathom how to secure your coop and run
• Understand the difference between free-range and fenced range

5 RAISE CHICKENS WITHOUT LAND (HOW TO)

Lots of people want to keep chickens but they live in the city or suburban areas with small backyards, and because of this they think they can't raise chickens because they don't have enough space. Keeping chickens when you have a small yard is a bit tricky, but it can be done with a good deal of planning and forethought.

Whilst typically the more room chickens have the better, there is always a way to get around having a small yard and this chapter will do exactly this by looking at how you can raise chickens in a small space.

Chicken Roaming Space and Basic Needs

The first thing you need to do is decide which type of chickens you would like: large fowl or bantams. The amount of space you have available to use will help to clarify this for you. Large birds such as Rhode Island Reds need four square feet of space per bird in the coop and about ten square feet of run or yard space. Smaller hens, such as bantams, need two square feet of coop per bird and eight square feet of run/yard. Obviously, you can fit more bantams into the available space, as they are generally half to one third the size of large fowl.

Remember though, bantam eggs will be appreciatively smaller than larger breeds. Chickens, unlike their owners, require just a few basic things to make the coop 'home'.

A roosting perch is needed. Although chickens will sleep on the floor, they feel safer if up higher.

An average of one nesting box for every three hens will suffice, but, it's better to use a 1:1 ratio. They can (and will) lay just about anywhere, but if you can persuade them to use a nesting box you won't have to search the coop and run for eggs. It also has the advantage of keeping the eggs away from chicken foot traffic which could result in broken eggs. If you are really tight on space you can remove the nesting boxes.

There should also be enough room to place a feeder. An inside feeder will deter rodents from an easy meal. If the coop area is 'tight' you could try using a wall mounted or corner feeder to save on space.

Water should be kept outside of the coop to maintain as low a humidity level as possible inside the coop. Too much humidity will encourage mold causing respiratory problems for the ladies.

Keeping the Coop Small

Is your coop going to be static in one place, or mobile? Static coops do not move around the yard. There are many available choices for you to pick from. To save space you need to go vertical! You can fit a decent sized coop; say four foot by six foot, in a modest sized yard by enclosing a run underneath the coop. This not only gives the hens some outside space, it also puts the coop at waist height for easy cleaning which is a bonus for anyone with back or leg problems.

A four foot by six foot coop gives you twenty-four square feet of floor space. Whether you want large hens or bantams, will determine the height and floor space you need and how many hens you can comfortably house. It is always tempting to add more hens but bear in mind that overcrowding can cause some pretty nasty anti-social behavior like bullying. The more room the hens have, the happier they will be.

If you have a small yard I would always recommend a mobile coop/chicken tractor. Chicken tractors are moveable coops. You can move them from one spot to another if you have enough available space. They will have a secure housing unit at one end with the run attached. It's ideal for small numbers of chickens. The only drawback to this type of coop as far as I can see, is in moving it. If you have a mobility or strength issue, it is going to be difficult for you to move the coop.

With a chicken tractor, when the hens have eaten all the grass in a certain patch the coop can be moved to another patch of grass. If you already have a static coop, you could consider buying a portable run which your girls could use during the daytime.

Buying the Perfect Small Coop

If you intend to buy a coop readymade or boxed, make sure you read the specs first. Many manufacturers of coops are 'optimistic' about how many hens can fit into their coop, if they say six, think four hens. Also be sure to check and see how well made they are. Will it withstand a predator trying to get in? How about the weather? There are some very cheap coops out there, and they are cheap for a reason!

The main downside of buying a readymade coop is they are generally in standard 'bulky' sizes- like six foot by four foot and if you have slim narrow yard this will be a problem. If you are handy or know a DIY enthusiast, it's fairly easy to make your own. Many people make coops out of recycled wood for a very reasonable price. You will probably have to buy some wood, screws and hardware, but you can build to your own particular needs and design.

Or, if you already have a small outbuilding, can you retro-fit it to house your girls? I know someone who shares her garden shed with her hens. Their area is sectioned off with access to the outside. It is a very safe and secure arrangement and a wonderful use of existing space.

Making Use of Existing Space: Indoor Chickens

You might be surprised to learn that many people keep one or two chickens as house pets! The birds will tend to have a dedicated area for their 'chicken activities' such as dust bathing, scratching and sleeping. The chicken as a 'house pet' is a great idea if you only want a couple of hens. They will faithfully lay you an egg and provide you with company and amusement.

Several people have therapy chickens. These birds help to stave off loneliness and anxiety. They have specifically been helpful in aiding autistic children's focus and helping them become less anxious and withdrawn. If you are thinking 'ewww' right about now imagining chicken poop on the carpet, there are chicken diapers! You could even make your own!

The idea of the coop in a chest of drawers could be utilized here very well. It would contain the eating and roosting area, leaving the bird to 'free range' in your house.

If you live in an apartment, you would have to choose a quiet, low profile chicken breed or the neighbors will get upset!

Chapter 5 Checklist

• Understand what a vertical coop and chicken tractor are
• Appreciate the difference between a small space and not enough space and
  • how this can effect chicken's behavior
  • Know how to make the most of whatever space you have

6 BRINGING YOUR CHICKS HOME (FOR THE FIRST TIME)

So you've worked out how much room your chickens need, designed your chicken coop and your chickens, chicks, or pullets are on the way. We can still remember the excitement of waiting for the delivery of our new chickens, our first question was: I wonder how long it will be until they lay their first egg? This chapter will detail what you need to do when they first arrive and how you can get them off to the best possible start in life.

Basic Chick Needs

Before your chicks arrive you will need to have a brooder box ready for them. This can be a modified plastic tote, cardboard box or similar container in which to house them. They need to be safe from predators (including the pet cat/dog), preferably in a fairly quiet, safe setting. If you have a garage or shed that is secure that will do nicely. Some folks set up the brooder in the house in a spare room or basement. If you consider having the chicks inside the house know that they will kick up a lot of dust, so if you have allergies this is not a good idea.

Figure 3: A homemade chicken brooder

You will need some sort of bedding for the chicks; it can be pine shavings, shredded newspaper, finely chopped straw or peat moss. The bedding should be absorbent, unscented and relatively inexpensive. The chicks will also need a chick sized feeder and drinker, the quantity you need will depend on how many chicks you get. A round screw on feeder will easily feed up to eight chicks and the same for the drinker. Finally, you will also need a heat source. This can be a heat lamp or a brooder plate. While the brooder plate is more expensive, it is infinitely safer.

Tip: If you have used a plastic tote for the brooder, you will need to put some burlap sacking under the shavings to help them grip and stand for at least the first couple of weeks.

Bringing Chicks Home

If you have mail ordered your chicks, you should be notified when they were shipped and when to expect them. Ideally the heat source should be running for a couple of hours before they arrive so that the temperature is perfect for them. If you are bringing them home from the store, turn the heat on immediately and check frequently for the first few hours. If they are scattered to the edges of the brooder it's too hot, if they are huddled under the lamp, too cold. Adjust the temperature until they are scattered around the brooder. The actual temperature on a thermometer should read between ninety and ninety five Fahrenheit. This should be reduced by five to ten degrees each week, until week six when the temperature should be around sixty five Fahrenheit.

Figure 4: Chicks in a small homemade Chicken Brooder

When you are putting the chicks in their new home for the first time, you will need to dip their beaks in the water briefly so they know where the water is.

Tip: Do not place the water under the heat lamp as they will not drink hot water.

You will need to show them where the food is. This can be achieved by scattering a few crumbles by the food dispenser. Don't be surprised if after they have drank and eaten they fall asleep, it has been a busy and confusing day for them and you should let them sleep.

Handling your Chicks

Over the next few days and weeks it's important that you know how and when you should be handling your chicks. This is a crucial stage in the bonding process and will help to establish the relationship you have with them throughout their life.

Chicks and Children

Children usually want to hold and cuddle cute, fluffy little things. Ensure they do this gently since the respiratory system of a bird is much different to ours. Chickens have air sacs distributed around their bodies as well as lungs. If they are held or squeezed too tightly they can suffocate very quickly. Children also should not be allowed to chase or harass the chicks, imagine how terrifying it must seem to the chick. If the chick grows up frightened of humans, you are not going to have a great rapport with your flock.

Getting to Know You

Chicks do not come ready to hop into your hand, so you have to spend time getting to know each other, look upon it as a 'date'. Start out by placing your hand on the floor of the brooder with some food in the palm, as long as you keep still they will come to investigate. After a couple of days doing this they should be unafraid of your hand, so try stroking them gently as they sit or stand on your hand. By the end of the week they should associate your hand with good things and be comfortable with you.

Continue the slow progress with picking them up briefly and rewarding them when you put them down. You can extend the time you hold them each day. Eventually they will come to you for picking up and a reward.

Moving from the Brooder to the Coop

At around six to eight weeks they should have their first full set of feathers and so will be able to maintain their own temperature at a constant level. This is the best time to move them from the brooder into the coop. A further caveat to moving them is; are they going to be on their own? If you plan to put them in with bigger birds they need to be at least two thirds the size of the adult birds.

They need to be able to escape from larger birds who will likely try to peck or harass the little ones. One way to help them is to provide plenty of room for them to escape to, perches that are higher up so they can fly to safety help too.

If you want to get them outside before integrating them with an existing flock then set up a safe, caged area where the chicks can get used to the outside noises and sights. I do this with most of my chicks; they go out in the morning and are put back to the brooder at night. This also helps them get used to being handled.

When they are ready to move outside permanently make sure to leave them locked up inside their coop for the first 24 hours. The reason behind leaving them locked in their coop for the first 24 hours is that they will realize that the coop is their home. Then when you eventually let them out into the pen, they will happily return to the coop to roost in the evenings.

Tip: Make sure to scatter some feed and provide water in the coop before locking them up for 24 hours.

Exploring their Environment

Chicks by nature are curious but cautious. Chicks are not as cautious as adults because they have yet to learn the dangers of the world. Once they are big enough to come out of the brooder box into their own coop, it's up to you to ensure that it is safe for them. It has to be predator proof and hold all the things necessary for chicks to thrive. Make sure there aren't any tight spaces where a chick might get stuck; curiosity can lead them to make some silly moves at times. They will explore their new home slowly at first, but should be comfortable by the second day. Be sure to make perches/roosting bars at chick height initially, they can be raised as needed later on. If you intend to free range your birds, it's best that they know where the coop is and understand that it is home, so keep them confined for about a week or so until they have got the hang of the routine.

Introducing Them to Their Pen

Once they've spent 24 hours in their coop it's time to introduce them to their pen/run for the first time. This is always an exciting moment and a great opportunity to get a really good view of your new chickens. It's important at this point to say don't force your chickens out of their coop. All you need to do is open their coop door and wait. For an added incentive you can spread some feed in their pen along with fresh water. If you're not sure what to feed them, read our beginners guide to feeding chickens.

The more curious chickens will leave the coop first and explore but within a few minutes the rest of the flock should come out and join them. If after a few hours the flock is still inside the coop give them a gentle push out into the pen. You can leave your chickens for the rest of the day now to explore their new environment and get comfortable!

When it starts to get dark it's important you go back outside and make sure your chickens are inside their coop. We've always found that by getting the chickens used to the coop (before they are allowed in the pen) they are much more likely to go back into the coop when it's dusk.

If your chickens aren't in their coop yet gently move them towards the coop (we do this by using a large sheet of wood 8×6 foot). Have a person at either end of the wood and drag the wood across the floor, moving the chickens back towards their coop. It's important that any move you make around the chickens is calm and slow; don't charge at them with the wood whatever you do!

You may find that for the following week or so your chickens need to be encouraged to leave the coop in the morning and go back to it during dusk. As previously mentioned, to do this, just leave the coop door open and sprinkle food out in the pen.

First Free Range Outings

After a week or so they will leave and return to their coop on their own and your chickens will be settling in nicely. It's at this point that if you are planning on letting your chickens free range, you can take down your temporary pen and let them roam! Again though, after their first day of free ranging, make sure they return back to their coop during the evening.

Letting them out to range can be nerve wracking for you the first few days, so make a small area in which they can move around in and get a 'feel' for the outdoor life. At roosting time they will probably put themselves to bed, if not, bribery is in order. Mealworms have to be the chickens' most favorite treat, so call them in with mealworms and shut the door after the last one arrives. Once they and you are comfortable with the routine, you can let them roam further afield. Although free ranging is ideal for the chicks, be very observant for hawks and other predators. Unfortunately chicks and young hens are prime targets for dinner. The best overall solution is to leave them in a covered run when you cannot be around to watch them.

The run need not seem like prison for them, perches at varying heights, a chicken swing and an old ladder to climb up will all help to keep them learning and busy. Ensure there is enough water out in the run area for them and plenty of feed in the coop. It is wise to not put chicken feed outside since it will attract vermin such as rats and mice. If feasible it would be great to have the run partially sunshaded so they can retreat from the hot sun as they need, also put the water in the shady part.

When you let them out to free range is a personal choice. I prefer later rather than earlier for a few reasons:
- The older they are the more cautious they are
- Larger size makes them not quite so easy to 'pick off'
- They are more familiar with their surroundings

Once they are around twelve to sixteen weeks they should be able to free range for themselves. As sixteen weeks is the start of the laying cycle for a few breeds, be on the lookout for eggs in strange places such as under the rose bush, hedgerow or in plain sight. If they continue to lay outside it might be beneficial to confine them for a few days to teach them where the egg is supposed to go. You can use fake eggs in the nest boxes to encourage them to use the boxes. Most of them will get with the program, but there is always one…

Occasionally they will decide to sleep in the nest boxes. This should be discouraged as they will poop while asleep and leave a mess to be cleaned up daily unless you want filthy eggs. Make sure the roosts are away from the boxes, if that can't be done, simply close the nesting boxes at night. Placing a piece of cardboard over the entrance will do the trick.

Chapter 6 Checklist

- Prepare for the arrival of your chicks
- Know how to handle your chicks
- Understand when to move them from the brooder to the coop
- Know what to look for during their first few free range outings.

7 PROVIDING FOOD AND WATER

Feeding your chickens is one of, if not, the most important task when it comes to raising backyard chickens. Get it right and you will have a healthy flock who merrily cluck every time you bring them one of their favorite snacks or kitchen scraps! Get it wrong, and it can lead to reduced egg production, deformed eggs, feather picking and other unwanted behavior.

No one chicken is the same, as each breed all require slightly different mixes of nutrition, as do laying birds or meat birds. Let's start at the beginning and work our way through what to feed your chickens, how to store their feed, providing water for your hens, how you should be feeding your chickens and finally which snacks and treats you can feed your hens.

Feed Choices

When standing in front of the feed stacks in the store it can be confusing and overwhelming to know which feed do my birds need? You will no doubt notice that companies often have a choice of what seems to be the same thing. This is where reading the label comes in handy! As a general rule of thumb, if the feed is a bit more expensive it will have more additives such as vitamins and minerals. This is certainly more important in younger birds and birds that are kept in a restricted area, but older hens that free range will likely find all the vitamins and minerals they need by scratching around in the yard.

Let's now go through the nutrition and feed requirements of a hen from birth to old age.

0-6 Weeks

Young chicks should be fed chick starter, this has 20% protein which is vitally important for those first few weeks. Chicks grow phenomenally quickly which is why they need a very high level of protein for the first six weeks. Starter feed can be medicated, which means amprolium has been added, or non-medicated. If you have older chickens as well as chicks it is best to use medicated, as the amprolium will help to protect them against coccidiosis.

Figure 5: Chick Crumb Feed

What is coccidiosis? It is a parasitic protozoa that lives in the gut of chickens. When a chicken has immunity the organism is kept under control, but when a bird is immuno-compromised, or as in the case of a young chick, has no resistance the infection can become overwhelming and lead to death. If you have not had your chicks vaccinated, it's wise to give them medicated feed for the first few weeks. The chicks will have built up immunity by around six weeks.

Meat birds will need even more protein than egg laying hens. There is a specially formulated feed called meat bird starter for these chicks which contains 22-24% protein.

6-10 Weeks

At ten weeks old they should be changed over to a

starter/grower mix which is 18% protein. We are now slowing their rate of growth slightly. They should be almost completely feathered out by now, so their protein requirement is slightly less.

Meat birds will require 18-20% feed after six weeks. They will continue on that formulation until slaughter.

10-18 Weeks

As the chicks reach around 10 weeks of age, they should be moved onto a grower/finisher mix of around 16% protein. The birds are coming into adulthood and laying soon. The growth process is almost finished now and it won't be long until they start laying eggs for you!

18 Weeks

When your hens reach 18 weeks of age they will be preparing to start laying eggs. At this age they need to be on a layers mix of around 16% protein in order to maintain good health. Your chickens should now be kept on this feed for the remainder of their life unless there are exceptional circumstances such as molts which will be discussed later in this chapter.

The only time you should move an older hen off layers mix is when they molt. During their molt you can purchase 'feather fixer' which is slightly higher in protein (18%) and contains herbal additives to give sheen and luster to the feathers. Once the molt is about done, change back to layer ration.

Tip: The above timings can be slightly changed around, but make sure to always feed enough protein to developing chicks.

In many areas your feed store will only stock starter, starter grower and layer mix. In practice you can feed chicks older than six weeks starter grower until they are eighteen to twenty weeks when you will switch to layer feed.

Now you know what you should be feeding your chickens and when, let's take a look at the variety of choices you have with their feed, where to purchase it and which variety to choose from.

Commercial feeds are by far the most common choice amongst backyard chicken keepers and they are the bags of feed which you see for sale at your local feed store. Feed manufacturers spend thousands, if not millions of dollars on researching the best possible recipe for poultry health in every stage of development; this is to ensure that you get healthy hens that are also productive. If you are new to raising backyard chickens and are looking for the simplest and easiest way to get started this is the option for you.

Organic Feed

In general this is quite a bit more expensive than the regular commercial feed you can buy. It is made from grain that have been grown organically with no pesticides or growth enhancers used. If you intend to raise your flock organically, or market them as organic, this is the feed you should use.

Tip: When purchasing organic feed a local feed mill is often cheaper than a 'big box' farm store.

Homemade Feed

Some 'old timers' will swear that their own recipe is the best for bird, maybe it is, maybe it isn't but mixing feed in the right quantities is tricky and certainly not recommended for beginner backyard chicken keepers. I would only recommend this approach to someone if they are experienced and raise a lot of chickens.

Fermented Feed

Fermenting feed is very good for the chickens, as it helps them to 'unlock' the nutrients inside of seeds and makes them more available to be used by the bird. Any feed or grain that you can feed to your hens, can be fermented. In its simplest form, you add water, a little apple cider vinegar and around ¼ teaspoon of yeast to the feed and store it in a suitable container (not metal). Over a period of about 3-4 days, your feed will smell vaguely like a sourdough. At this stage it is ready for your chickens to eat. It can easily be done at home as there is no special equipment you will need. You will however need a warm area for it to ferment in. Most folks run fermentation in a three day cycle so that there is always one ready for the next day. Again though, I would only recommend this approach to someone if they are experienced and raise a lot of chickens.

Water

Water is essential to all living things and chickens are no exception. Chicks and chickens need constant access to clean, fresh water (yes, they love to drink out of muddy puddles too). A hen will drink about a cup of water each day. She will take frequent small sips throughout the day. Too little water can affect egg production among many other things, so make sure they have plenty. There are approximately fifteen cups of water to one US gallon, so if you have a lot of birds you will need a couple of drinkers for them. As an example I have around forty birds and I put out four drinkers in various places, which ensures they all have access to water.

You can place the water in any sort of plastic container, but the easiest way is to buy a drinker.

Tip: During the winter if you live in a colder climate, the water will probably freeze over during the evenings, so just make sure to break the ice up and clean out the bowl in the mornings. If you have bad winters, I highly recommend you invest in some sort of heated drinker.

Other Nutrients and Requirements

Calcium

Laying hens need a constant source of calcium to help with the formation of eggshells, maintenance of bones and feather health. Calcium can be given as oyster shell or recycled eggshells. Oyster shell is readily available at a feed store and it should be given separately from their feed as too much calcium can cause problems. Just sprinkle it on the ground and your hens will help themselves when they need it.

If you have to feed them recycled eggshells instead they need baking beforehand. Eggshells can be baked for fifteen minutes in a hot oven then left to cool. After the eggshells have cooled, you should crush them finely and then feed them to your hens.

Grit

Once the bird starts to free range she should be given grit. Chick grit is finely ground for chicks and is useless to adult birds, so make sure you buy the correct pack at your feed store. Grit is taken into the gizzard where it sits and helps to grind down food into a paste for easier digestion. If you don't give them grit you run the risk of a hen getting an impacted crop which can be fatal.

Supplements

There are a whole host of supplements you can give your chicken, but only two of them are important enough to be mentioned here. The first is electrolyte solution or powder. This can be easily added to a drinker when the need arises. I use this twice a week in hot weather. Although chickens cannot sweat, they will increase their water intake which in turn can give them diarrhea. The diarrhea will wash vital electrolytes from the system before they have been absorbed from the food, so it's important to replace them.

The second supplement is for gut health and it's called probiotic. There are several different kinds out there so choose which you prefer. I give this about once a month or if the birds have been stressed for any reason.

Folk Remedies

There are many, many folk remedies for chickens out there, so many that it would not be possible to list them all here - we would need a separate book. However, one that is currently very popular is the addition of Apple Cider Vinegar to the water. While I don't believe the addition of ACV to be necessarily harmful, there really is no evidence to suggest that it is helpful either. Personally, I do add ACV to their water once a week in wintertime only. It is said to be helpful to the normal gut flora, some also claim it reduces the amount of salmonella and campylobacter in the birds gut.

Tip: If you do come across a folk remedy, research it before you practice on the birds. Some remedies are ill advised at best and dangerous for your hens.

Storing your Feed and Supplies

If you have chickens already, it's likely you have mice, rats or chipmunks helping themselves to your feed. If you are really unlucky, you have all three. Rodents are great at freeloading and increasing the size of their family, so you will need to keep your feed and supplements in vermin proof containers. Plastic trash cans and tote bins both make good containers. They are lightweight and easy to clean out; the only problem is that eventually rodents may chew through the plastic. Check your plastic containers for holes each time you refill them and if there are any signs of entry - move the bin or replace it. Metal bins can also be used although I have heard complaints that the metal 'sweats' in summer dampening the feed and causing mold issues. Whichever container you decide to use, the feed needs to be stored in a cool, dry place where it can't be contaminated.

Your containers don't have to be huge, as you should store only enough to get you through a month or so. Feed that is stored for a long time loses some of the vitamins and can go moldy, two months should be the maximum time you store feed.

Your packets of supplements can easily be stored in a glass container or kept in the house. Multi-dose items such as electrolyte powder need to be kept somewhere dry otherwise it will turn into a solid block of powder.

How Much and When do I Feed Them?

The easiest way to feed your hens is known as free choice. Free choice means that your hens always have access to feed and decide themselves when and how much to eat.

To do this you need to buy a large feeder and hang it inside the coop. You then just fill the feeder up and each evening top up the feeder. This way the hens can help themselves when they want; this saves you from worrying that the food has run out. The average hen will eat about a quarter pound of feed each day, slightly more in winter and less in summer. There are other variables that affect intake also including; broodiness, stress and molting.

Figure 6: A traditional chicken feeder

Some folks put out only enough feed for each bird daily. There is nothing wrong with this approach as long as the birds are getting enough nutrition from their food. If there is a truly bossy hen in the flock, she may prevent the others from eating their fill. If you are feeding your hens daily then you should do this once in the morning and once in the evening - remember they like to eat small portions but often. The only downside of daily feeding is it also time consuming for the busy keeper, since you have to measure out feed in the morning and again in the evening. This may seem pleasant enough… until the snow flies! Over time you will learn exactly how much feed your chickens need and this will depend on the breed, how active they are and the time of the year. If you are constantly finding feed in the trough then reduce the amount you give them slightly more.

Once you've decided if you're going to feed them as free choice or just enough feed each day you need to decide what to place the feed in. Whilst you can just scatter the feed on the floor this isn't recommended as it attracts vermin. The two most common choices are feeders or trough, both of which help to keep the feed clean and dry. Generally if you are going with the free choice option you use a feeder, or if you just want to give them enough food each day then you use a trough.

Figure 7: A traditional chicken trough

Tip: Generally free-range chickens won't over eat so you can't over face them. If you put too many pellets in their feeder they simply won't eat them.

A final note on feeding. Ensure you have a sufficient number of drinkers and feeders for your flock. There is always a 'top hen' who will think the drinker and feeder are her personal property and will chase away the more timid flock members. Since drinkers and waterers are fairly inexpensive, if you have over six hens buy two of each. If you are inventive you can make your own. They don't need to be works of art, just functional.

Treats and Prohibitions

When your hens line up at the gate waiting for you to come with some treats, it's very hard to resist them! Treats are fine as long as they are healthy and given in moderation. Treats should make up no more than five percent of their daily intake. Obesity brings its' own troubles including laying problems so try and keep those ladies trim and healthy.

- Mealworms are a chickens' number one treat. Mealworms are high in protein, so the quantity should be limited since too much protein can cause kidney problems. A teaspoon per hen should be ample, although the hens will tell you differently!
- Fruits such as bananas, berries, strawberries (hugely popular), and perhaps the all-time favorite watermelon. Watermelon is especially good for them on those hot, steamy days of summer. Chop up the watermelon, add water and freeze. Put them out for the hens and watch them peck contentedly for ages. You can do the same for almost anything on this list.
- In the winter I make an oatmeal gruel to which I add a large dollop of plain yoghurt and a sprinkle of oregano herb. The oatmeal gives them a quick boost of carbohydrates and helps to keep them warm.
- Stale bread, if it's really hard then soak it in water for a while before feeding to the hens.
- Veggies such as kale, broccoli and cabbage are all great sources of vitamins for them.
- Scratch grains is a mixture of corn, milo, oats, barley and wheat. The mix is low in protein and fiber so it should only be used as a treat. Many people give their birds scratch before bedtime in the winter since the high carbohydrate level will digest slowly and keep them warm.
- Corn (whole or cracked), as noted with scratch grain, corn is high in carbohydrate and low in protein so should only be used as a wintertime treat.

Absolutely Not For Chickens!

There are some things chickens should not have since they are poisonous or detrimental to their health. The following is general list, so like all things chicken: if in doubt don't give it to your flock until you research it.

- Any moldy produce. Would you eat it? If no, then the chickens shouldn't eat it either.
- Alcohol
- Chocolate
- Salty products can cause issues with the kidneys, so no potato chips please!
- Uncooked beans

• Avocado- they can eat the flesh but not the skin or pit. To avoid confusion, don't feed it to them.

• Apple seeds contain minute amounts of cyanide; remove them from the apple before giving them to your flock.

Chapter 7 Checklist

• Know the difference between chicken feeds and which is best for your chicks

• Understand when to feed your hens and how

• Know what additional nutrients your hens require

• Recognize which types of food you should never give to your hens

8 LAYING HEN MANAGEMENT

Managing your laying flock may sound like its complex, but in reality it's fairly simple to do. The hen does all the work and you take care of her needs. However, there are certain things you should know before you get overwhelmed by hiccups in the process. Hens will lay an egg once every twenty five to twenty seven hours, so roughly one egg per day. She will lay slightly later each day until her body skips an egg. Why does it do that? In this chapter we are going to talk you through how to keep your hens laying eggs and how to manage any problems that may occur along the way.

Internal Factors that Affect Egg Laying

When a pullet reaches laying age, somewhere around the eighteen to twenty week mark she will start her laying cycle. The first eggs a pullet will lay will be smaller than a hen who has been laying for a while. It may also be misshapen or 'defective' in some way. That is acceptable in a young bird, as it takes time to get the machinery running smoothly. The first one to two years of production are the most prolific and after two years the amount of eggs will decrease slowly over the years. Hens laying until seven or eight years or more are unusual, but not unheard of.

How long your hen keeps laying is dependent on the breed you have. Many of the 'production' hens are spent after three years at most. Commercial farmers will cull the flock and replace with new stock. Heritage breeds will lay for longer, although not in the prolific amounts of production hens.

Let's now look at what internal factors can affect a hens egg laying.

Molting

Pullets will not molt the first year. After fifteen to eighteen months they will have completed their first laying cycle and they will molt in their second winter. It is said the best layers molt earlier and quicker in order to come back into production. There is nothing you can do to prevent molting. You can however supply good quality feed with a slightly higher protein level around eighteen per cent. Be sure to give them vitamins and electrolytes in their water once a week and ensure they have plenty of calcium to eat.

Figure 8: A young hen molting

Parasites

Parasites include intestinal worms, lice and mites. If the parasite load is small, it is symbiotic with the hen, but when the parasites multiply rapidly they can drain a hen of nutrition and also cause anemia. Frequent health checks will help to avoid this from happening. Many folks worm and dust their flock on a timetable, others prefer to treat only when there is a problem. There really is nothing wrong with either approach, just do what fits best for you and parasites won't affect your egg production.

Disease
There are a number of infectious diseases that will cause a drop in egg production. Many of these diseases will pass without treatment such as avian coryza otherwise known as the common cold. Others such as fowl pox, coccidiosis, infectious bronchitis and avian influenza require a more aggressive stance. Antibiotics are the drug of choice and should be prescribed by your veterinarian. Many people medicate their flock with an antibiotic bought from a farm store. If treated with the wrong antibiotic the hen will not get better and the virus/infection may become resistant to several antibiotics which can create even more problems.

External Factors that Affect Egg Laying

Not only can internal factors affect egg laying but external factors can also affect it too. There are several factors that can influence how often a hen will lay. The easiest to monitor and rectify are feed and water.

Feed and Water
Once they commence laying they will need a sixteen per cent protein, high quality feed. It is extremely important for them to have the correct feed. Many people try to cut costs by mixing their own feed, which is fine if you are a chicken nutritionist, but most folks do not correctly make homemade rations. The feed companies spend millions of dollars on feed research and feed is precisely mixed with the correct amount of additives. At twelve to fifteen dollars for a fifty pound bag, unless you have a large flock it really isn't financially worth mixing your own feed.

A hen must have access to cool, fresh water at all times, if she cannot drink, she will not lay regularly. The water needs to be cool otherwise if the temperature of the water is too warm, she likely will not drink as much as she should. To avoid this, place several drinking stations in several locations that are situated in the shade.

It is the same thing with feed. If laying hens are not fed an appropriate feed it will influence the amount and quality of her eggs. At eighteen to twenty weeks a hen should be gradually switched from finisher to layer feed which is sixteen per cent protein. If you have a flock of various ages from chick to older hen, you can use eighteen per cent until the chicks reach the laying point.

Calcium

Hens also need additional calcium that they can access anytime they want. This extra calcium helps to keep her bones sturdy and provide good, strong eggshells. Without this calcium eggshells will become thin like parchment or even nonexistent. The hens' body will leach calcium from her bones to make eggshells, so her bones will become brittle causing fractures in extreme cases. Please follow the calcium guidance in Chapter 6 for more advice.

Poisoning

Poisoning is usually accidental and is not common in backyard flocks. One of the biggest culprits is moldy or contaminated feed. Another source of mycotoxin is moldy bedding, which is why you should not store hay/straw bales inside the coop during the winter. When the material gets damp, mold spores form and create the mycotoxins that poison the hen.

Another fairly frequent poison is botulism. A dead carcass of a mouse or similar, can be pecked at by chickens and they ingest the neurotoxin created by the bacteria. If you compost small carcasses in the compost heap do not allow the chickens to dine there.

Nest Boxes

Have you got enough nest boxes for your hens? You should provide one nest box for every three hens. If you don't have sufficient boxes they will find an alternative place to lay, which means you will be searching for impromptu nests everywhere they are allowed to go. The nest box for a heavy breed hen should be roughly twelve inches square and lined with nest material such as straw or shredded newspaper.

Tip: Since eggs do get broken occasionally, place a square of cardboard under the nesting material. When it gets mucky, just toss it out and replace!

Sudden Decrease in Egg Laying

If you are used to collecting a dozen a day and suddenly find you are only collecting five or six, you will have to become a detective to find out what's going on. Sometimes you have a predator problem, such as snakes and rats stealing eggs, so make sure there isn't a place where they can gain access to the coop. Do you have an egg eater among your flock? Occasionally an egg will get broken in the nest and the hen will eat it. This can be solved by frequent collection of eggs, or using a 'roll-away' system for the nest boxes. The egg will gently roll away from the hen as she lays it so it's not available to eat.

Do you have pastured chickens? If so, you may have a couple of them laying in hidden places. This has happened on many occasions, sometimes the hen disappears to return with chicks following! Check under bushes and shrubs, look in small darkened places where she might be hiding them.

Figure 9: Finding a secret stash of eggs

Daylight

A change in the seasons can cause a sudden drop in egg laying. Hens require around fourteen to sixteen hours of daylight to complete the egg formation and laying. As the daylight get shorter, you will definitely notice a decrease in the number of eggs that are laid. This is perfectly natural as it gives your hen's body a chance to recover during the winter.

Tip: If you still want your hens to lay during this time then read our section below on controlled lighting.

Stress or Changes in their routine

Hens are creatures of habit, so if you make any changes to their routine you are likely to throw them off laying for a bit. It can be something simple like moving a feeder or moving coops around that affects perhaps one or two timid members of the flock. Larger changes such as moving them completely to another location are likely to cause some consternation among all of them. Don't worry; they will get back to business once the dust has settled.

Still Not Laying?

Occasionally you will get a hen that cannot lay, this can be due to birth defects or congenital defects. Many folks are cross breeding backyard stock with good results, but sometimes there are 'oddities' created.

More commonly you will have to deal with hens that have things like a prolapsed vent or egg yolk peritonitis. We will be going over these health issues in chapter nine.

Tip: If your hen still isn't laying an egg, be sure to email us and we will do our best to help!

Controlled Lighting

The hens' internal mechanism for laying eggs is governed by the amount of daylight she receives; she needs at least fourteen hours of light to keep on laying. Naturally during the summer months she receives plenty of light and so will lay regularly. What happens when the daylight starts to diminish? As the days get shorter, the hen is preparing to molt. During the molting process she will lose most of her feathers and replace them with new feathers. Since feathers are around eighty five per cent protein, she will stop laying eggs during the molt. Once the molt has finished, if there is sufficient light she will start laying again. However in the US during the winter months the average amount of daylight is only 9.5 hours.

This reduction in daylight gives the hens rest. It's important for the hen to have some time to rest her body. Some long time chicken keepers and veterinarians believe that continuous laying leads to either vent prolapse or ovarian cancer. I personally let my hens rest during the winter because I believe this is healthier for them in the long run. However what do you do if you want your hens to continue laying during the winter months? You must provide them with artificial lighting in the coop.

A 40w lightbulb (make sure you don't use a fluorescent lightbulb) provides enough light for a 10" x 10" coop. Make sure that the lightbulb is securely fitted; I'd also use a second fitting just in case the first fixing fails and your light falls onto the floor. For the fixing use either wire or chain metal, pests such as rats can chew through string. When fitting the light source make sure it's kept out of reach of the chickens and away from dry bedding/other potential flammable material.

Once the lightbulb is fitted, you can use a timer to set the lightbulb to come on from 4am-8am. The artificial light needs to be added in the morning as opposed to the evening to avoid stressing the birds. Throughout winter you need to match the sunset time to your artificial lightbulb timer to make sure your hens' daylight stays consistently at around 14 hours. So as we move further into winter, you will need to leave your lightbulb on longer to maintain the 14 hours a day. But as we get closer to February and the natural daylight starts getting longer, you will want to reduce the length of time you leave the lightbulb on for.

Collecting, Cleaning and Storing Eggs

Collecting eggs should be done at least twice a day. If eggs sit around for a while, hens can get inquisitive and break and eat them. This is a difficult habit to break, so it's better to not have it start. If an egg has broken in the nest, make sure you clean it up at once. Not only will hens come to investigate but it will start to smell after a day or so. We have already said that predators will steal eggs too; rats will take them away and snakes will eat them whole, so be vigilant.

Eggs do not need to be washed unless they are soiled. Ensuring nest boxes are clean will help to keep soiling to a minimum. If you do have to wash them though use warm/hot water, at least twenty degrees warmer than the egg. Make sure you just rub gently over the area to remove soiling. Why? When eggs are laid they are covered in a micro layer which is called 'the bloom'. The bloom serves to keep germs from entering into the egg. If you wash the egg, you are removing the bloom. Since the egg is porous, cold water will penetrate the shell through the pores, hot water will not so much.

After they have been washed you should refrigerate them, pointed end down to prevent any evaporation from the egg. Eggs can be stored for three months in the fridge, make sure they are in a carton or covered in some way. If you aren't sure whether or not the egg is good to eat try the float test. Gently drop the egg in a glass of water. If it is fresh it will sink to the bottom and 'stand up'. If it floats to the top then toss it out!

Tip: If you eat your eggs quickly, there is no need to refrigerate. England and the Continent usually do not store eggs in the fridge.

Chapter 8 Checklist

• Be able to understand internal and external factors that affect egg laying
• Know how to install artificial lighting into your coop

9 INTRODUCE NEW CHICKENS TO YOUR FLOCK (HOW TO)

I think we all get 'that' craving every time spring comes round, should we get a few more chicks!? In fact with our first flock, it didn't even take us this long, after the first weekend we went and got another six pullets. Before we knew it we had twelve pullets in our coop staring back at us!

Fortunately as the first six pullets were still establishing their pecking order, introducing six additional pullets was surprisingly easy and it happened without too much squabbling. Unfortunately this isn't always the case and introducing new chickens to your existing flock can be a distressing and problematic time for both you and your chickens. In this chapter we are going to talk you through how to add new chickens into your existing flock with minimal disturbance!

Quarantine New Chickens

Adult chickens are much more likely to be carrying a disease or infection, whereas chicks from a hatchery should be disease free. As a rule of thumb we say if you are introducing chicks or pullets from a reputable dealer, then quarantine isn't required.

The first step when introducing new chickens to your flock is quarantining the new chickens to ensure they don't have any infections or diseases. When you get your new chickens home, make sure you have a separate coop (or a large crate) prepared for them. From this separate coop you can observe them to check they are fit and disease free. The last thing you want to do is give your existing flock a disease from your new chickens.

The key things to look for are:
- Signs of lice or mites
- Dull/ shrivelled comb
- Blocked nostrils/ fluid coming from their eyes
- Scaly legs

If you are relatively new to raising chickens and are unsure what you are looking for, ask a more experienced friend to check your new chickens or failing that, head over to Chapter 3 , under section 'What should I look out for'?

Whilst your new chickens are quarantined it's a good idea to supplement their water with minerals to make sure they are fully fit before they meet your existing flock. Also, if you notice they look slightly underweight make sure to feed them well to get them strong and healthy before they meet your existing flock.

Quarantining should last anywhere from 7 to 31 days. The longer you quarantine your new chickens the safer it is for the existing flock, because you have more time to spot any illness/disease. During this quarantine period make sure you thoroughly wash your hands in-between visiting your new chickens and existing flock. This will prevent any disease and infections spreading between the two separate camps.

Introduce Your New Chickens Slowly

We can't stress this next point enough: don't rush introducing your new chickens. Even if your new chickens don't need quarantining, don't just place them straight in with your existing flock, as this will cause lots of unnecessary trouble and fighting. You need a period of time where your existing flock can see the new chickens but can't 'touch' them. The easiest way to achieve this is to place the new chickens in their own pen which is placed next to the existing pen. This way, your existing flock can get use to the new chickens without instantly squabbling.

Another popular method is to place a crate inside the existing pen and place your new chickens inside this crate. We've not used this technique as this is a more aggressive tactic. Whichever method you decide to use, it's important that for around a week your new chickens are visible but kept separate from your existing flock.

Give Your Chickens a Proper Introduction

After you have successfully quarantined and 'visually introduced' your new chickens it's time to physically introduce them to each other.

If your chickens free range, the best way to introduce them is let the new chickens out first to free range and then after a few minutes open the existing coop up and let your existing flock join the new chickens to free range. If your chickens don't free range and are in a pen then the same principal applies, place the new chickens in the pen first and then let your existing flock out to greet the new chickens.

When your existing flock 'greet' the new chickens you will find there will be some scraps and jostling as they establish the new pecking order. This is perfectly normal and is a necessary step when successfully introducing new chickens. You should only stop this jostling if one of the chickens looks injured or starts to bleed- you don't want your chickens to experience any permanent injuries. If you find that the jostling is getting more and more intense and it lasts more than several minutes, separate the new chickens and re-introduce them again tomorrow.

Tip: Continue to do this once a day until within a few minutes of introducing them, they have settled down.

You will find that each breed reacts to new chickens differently. Hybrids and Buff Orpington's are normally very laid back and welcome newcomers. However you may find that Silkies or Rhode Island Reds can be very territorial and don't take well to new chickens.

After the chickens have met and can stay outside together it's time for the final play: moving the new chickens from their crate and into the existing coop. You should find that after free ranging for the day the new chickens will follow the flock into the coop and settle themselves in. However, if this doesn't happen and they try to return to their old crate- let them. Then, during the night take the chickens out of their crate and place them into the existing coop.

How Long Will it Take to Introduce Them?

All of the steps above might seem time consuming and unnecessary to some backyard chicken keepers out there. However, in our experience it's better not to rush these things and make sure due diligence is paid.

Quarantining
This shouldn't last more than a month. This will give you plenty of time to effectively assess the new chickens and treat any illnesses which they may have.

Visual Introductions
A week here is plenty of time for the existing flock to get used to having the new chickens in their presence.

Physical Introductions
If you get lucky you will only need to do this once and they will be fine. However if you have a more aggressive/territorial breed of chicken it might take 3-4 attempts to successfully physically introduce them.

Settling In

After the chickens have been introduced you need to keep a close eye on them the following week. Make sure they are all eating and drinking properly and also keep an eye on egg production. Sometimes when you introduced new chickens to the flock they go off lay.

So in total you are looking at around 5-6 weeks from getting your new chickens home to fully integrating them into your existing flock.

Introducing Baby Chicks to Adults

If you let nature take its course and have a broody hen that hatches her own eggs, she will protect her own chicks. However if you buy an incubator and hatch your own chicks and try to introduce them into your existing flock you're going to have problems. For the first 15-16 weeks you need to separate the chicks and keep them in their own pen. You need to wait until the chicks have their feathers and are a similar size to the chickens in the existing flock. Once they are a similar size you can follow the process above without the quarantine stage.

Mixing Breeds

If you are intending to introduce different breeds into your flock then this can also cause some unique issues, with the main concern being the potential size difference. Larger breeds will always be more dominant so it isn't fair to introduce a smaller breed (i.e. Silkies) to a larger breed (i.e. Jersey Giant) as the larger breed will bully the smaller breeds. I know some backyard chicken keepers who have successfully integrated smaller and larger breeds into a flock but it can be difficult.

Tips and Tricks

• Relocate Both Flocks: If possible when you introduce the new chickens, move the existing coop and pen to a new area so the existing and the new chickens are starting with a new piece of land.

• Same Size Matters: Try to only introduce chickens which are a similar size to your existing flock.

• Extend Before you Introduce: Ensure there is enough room in your existing coop and pen before the introduction of new chickens.

• Isolate Aggressive Birds: If you notice one chicken in particular is being overly aggressive to the newcomers, place the aggressive chicken in isolation for a few days to put her in check.

• Distract With Treats: When you do physically introduce the new chickens make sure to have some treats at the ready to use as a distraction if needed.

• Don't Introduce Just One: Make sure you don't introduce just one new chicken. Instead introduce at least two new chickens so the jostling/bullying from the existing pack is spread between them.

Chapter 9 Checklist

• Understand how to introduce new chickens to your flock

10 COMMON CHICKEN PROBLEMS

U nfortunately it's likely that at some point during your chickens' life they will have some sort of problem, whether that be broodiness, predators or bullying. There are several common problems that occur when you have chickens. If you aren't prepared for them they can seem frightening or overwhelming. Here we will introduce you to the usual problems or issues that usually arise sooner or later and how you should handle them.

Molting

Molting is the process of losing all old, worn out feathers and replacing them with new plumage. It happens to all birds including roosters. Some birds can take up to two years to complete a molt, but the humble chicken is usually done in three months.

Chicks have two mini-molts before they reach adulthood. You really don't notice much because they are always covered with down or feathers or a combination of both. Adult chickens look like they have been plucked ready for the table! Adult birds will have their molt somewhere between twelve months and eighteen months, depending on when they were born. The molt follows a definite pattern in the bird, starting with the head and neck and traveling down to the body and wings with finally the tail going. Needless to say they look very tatty at this stage.

Fast molters may seem fine one day and then when you open the coop in the morning you have a semi-naked bird and a pile of feathers! If a hen molts fast she will regrow her feathers just as quickly and commence laying. As you know, feathers are made of proteins so during the molt, egg laying will slow dramatically and then stop. This is the bodies' way of channeling all the available protein into making new feathers.

Tip: You should give them a higher protein feed with at least eighteen percent while they are molting.

When a hen is molting, her new 'pin' feathers are growing at the same time, giving her a hedgehog appearance sometimes. Please try to avoid picking up your hens when they are molting. The pin feathers are incredibly sensitive and it will hurt her if you pick her up.

Figure 10: A hen beginning their molt

Broodiness

What is a broody hen? You will know it when you see it! She will sit in the nest constantly, if anyone approaches her she will grumble, squawk and puff herself up, she may give you an almighty peck too. She may or may not be sitting on eggs, if she is, she likely stole some of her sisters' eggs too. This is a hormonal driven instinct to raise chicks which happens in the spring and summer months. However, some breeds of chickens are prone to broodiness, with Silkies coming to mind as broody queens. Many of the backyard breeds we have today have had the 'broodiness' bred out of them, however, there are always exceptions to every rule. Recently I have had four Rhode Island Reds broody, they certainly aren't known for their broody traits.

Broodiness can be a good or bad thing depending on what you want from your flock. Many folks simply want eggs, so broodiness is not good for them. When a hen goes broody she will not lay any eggs until she has hatched and raised those eggs which she is sitting on. This can be a couple of months. If however, you want to increase flock size but don't want an incubator expense, a broody hen will do the job for you very nicely and much cheaper too.

During her broody time, she will eat and drink infrequently and only leave the nest to poop, maybe a quick dust bath and then right back to it. Some are so neurotic about it they forget to eat and drink and so need to be reminded. A small dish of water soaked pellets will usually entice them to eat.

Figure 11: A broody hen in the nesting box

Well you have lots of options and you can break her broodiness without doing any emotional damage to her so don't worry! Let's look at some of the easier options which should work in most cases.

Remove Her From The Nesting Box

Pick the broody hen up out of her nest and drop her off with the rest of the chickens in the pen. You can do this the same time as you're feeding them for maximum effect. Also as we previously noted, broody hens can bite so make sure to wear gloves when you're doing this. Keep an eye on the hen because she might go straight back to the nest box. Repeat this step several times each day to try and 'break' her.

Block Off The Nesting Box

If she keeps returning to the nesting box after several days, it's time to up the ante. Remove her from the nesting box, like you've already been doing, except once she's out block the specific nesting box she's staying in- just nail a piece of wood to the entrance. Also remove the nesting straw out of the box to further dampen her spirits just in case she does break back in!

Make Her Roost Again

If she's still broody you have one stubborn girl but don't worry, we still have some more tricks up our sleeves. Just as its going dark and your hens are going back to the coop to roost, take your broody hen from her nest and place her with the other chickens roosting. Chances are she won't be brave enough to risk moving in the dark back to the nesting box.

Use Frozen Vegetables

At this point we've always managed to break our hen's broodiness however, other backyard chicken owners haven't been this fortunate so what else can you do? I've heard several people have placed a bag of frozen vegetables underneath their hen. They do this because when a hen is broody their body temperature rises so reducing it (with the frozen vegetables) will sometimes send a message to their brain that they aren't broody anymore.

Bullying

The pecking order is so called for a reason. Each and every bird in a flock will have their own place. Those at the top get to eat first, those at the bottom eat last. It is a very simple but effective hierarchy so that all members know their position. The pecking order can be somewhat fluid; a hen can move up the 'corporate' ladder or be demoted to the bottom. All of this depends on an individual's breed characteristic and attitude.

Bullying does occur to a small degree each day. If a chicken goes out of turn she gets a quick peck to the head to remind her of her status. This is usually where it ends, but sometimes it will turn ugly and you will have to intervene. New flock members will be harassed until they have been assimilated into the flock. They will usually start at the bottom but if one decides she isn't going to back down there can be quite a tussle for placement. Peck wounds and feather plucking can get out of hand and once a bird is injured all the flock members will likely pick on the injured bird. It sounds awful, but in the wild an injured bird is a liability to the flock and will either remove herself or be removed.

If the hen is bleeding you will need to remove her quickly. Her wounds will need to be cleaned up and she will have to be isolated until she heals. Once healed, you can try re-integration again but very slowly and only under your watchful eye. For the above reasons you should never introduce a single bird to the flock if you can help it because she will get everyone's attention.

Predators

Even if you live in the middle of the city, there will be a chicken predator in your neighborhood. Foxes, coyotes, raccoons and the 'pet' dog down the road will likely all want chicken dinner and these are only the ground predators. Owls and hawks also eat chicken when available. The key to your flocks' safety is coop security and awareness of predatory animals and the area in which you live.

Your coop and run needs to be predator proof or you risk losing your hens. Never, ever leave the coop door open at night even if it's within a run, use locks that require the ability of opposable thumbs to open such as a snap lock. Raccoons are incredibly smart and dexterous with locks.

Foxes, coyotes and dogs will try to dig under the run. If your coop is 'fixed' you can prevent this by burying the perimeter wire into the ground by about six inches. The bottom of a chicken tractor can be covered with hardware cloth if you have a high predator load in your area.

Aerial predators can be discouraged by stringing a network of tapes or wires across the top of the run if it's open at the top. This disrupts the 'flight path' and hinders both attack and escape. If you want your birds to have some shade, as well as protection, you could use a tarp sheet instead of chicken wire.

If you are fortunate enough to have a large garden, make sure you cut down any tall grass, bush or overgrown areas within 50-75 feet of your coop. The less cover a predator has, the more vulnerable they are at being seen before attacking. This will thwart less confident predators, as they won't risk exposing themselves to attack.

Weather Related Problems

Chickens are usually very hardy and tolerant of a wide variety of weather related problems. Problems start to occur when the weather becomes extreme such as heat waves and bitterly cold, wet winters. With a little foresight it's relatively easy to avoid major issues with the flock.

Extreme Heat

Extreme heat here is defined as sudden heat waves rather than a constant of the area in which you live. Chickens will acclimate to just about any environment they are raised in. Recently many states have seen record high temperatures, which means chickens will need shade to rest in. If you don't have shade available to them you can improvise by putting up shade cloth or tarps as a temporary barrier to the sun. Water is also a huge necessity and must be available at all times. A chicken will normally drink about a cup of water per day, in extreme heat this can increase to three cups. They also will like a dust bathing area so they can lie in the cool dirt and take care of parasites. Lice, ticks and mites thrive in hot weather so check your hens for infestation weekly.

Heat Stroke

Chickens can get heat stroke easily, this is an emergency and requires quick action to save your hen. ΄ If a hen is lying unresponsive or lethargic act immediately. She will need to be cooled down with cool water, if needed you can stand her in it up to her neck for a couple of minutes. Ensure the feathers are damp and the water reaches the skin. Towel her gently when you take her out. Offer cold treats such as iced watermelon, she needs to replace lost fluids. Encourage her to take small sips and keep her somewhere cool until she is back to her baseline. Occasionally hens will suffer neurological damage and can take months to heal.

Extreme Cold

Chickens can actually deal better with the cold weather. They have lots of warm insulation called feathers! They can and do have problems with the cold if they live in a drafty coop. Chickens can tolerate temperatures down to twenty below Fahrenheit without too much hardship. Once the mercury plummets lower for an extended period you may need to think about adding some sort of heat conservation for them. It is best to use an oil filled radiator firmly attached to the floor or wall, as heat lamps are dangerous and improper hanging or fixation of them can easily cause a coop fire. To check the temperature inside your coop, place a thermometer in the center overnight. In the morning check the reading, if it's between thirty two and forty two Fahrenheit, they do not need heat.

Frostbite

If there is a cold, damp draft blowing on them overnight, they can develop frostbite on their combs and wattles. The birds worst affected are those with large combs and wattles such as roosters. Frostbite can also occur with inadequate ventilation in the coop. When chickens exhale there is moisture in their breath, chicken poop also contains moisture. This moisture is chilled quickly by the cold wind and turns to ice on the surfaces it touches, such as a large comb. Initially the comb will look pale white in appearance it may feel warm to the touch. In second degree frostbite the comb will feel like 'frozen chicken', it may blister and swell. In third degree frostbite the comb will feel waxy and hard, it will slowly blacken and drop off. The loss of comb and wattles is significant because the birds thermo-regulate using the comb and wattles, so it will impair this ability badly. The legs and feet can also be affected by frostbite so keep a very close eye on your birds, check them daily as necessary.

Preventing frostbite is fairly easy, you need to ensure there are no drafts in the coop, no drinkers in the coop. Perches should be sufficiently wide so they can sit on their feet and keep them warm. If they do get frostbite, remember to warm the area gradually and don't rub it or pop the blisters. Don't apply direct heat to the area, ensure they are eating and drinking well. If you think it's necessary, remove the bird to a warmer area so you can do a thorough check.

In severe cases you will need to contact your veterinarian.

Tip: During an especially cold night you can put Vaseline or similar on the comb and wattles for overnight protection.

How to Hold Chickens Safely

Unless it's essential that you pick them up for something, try to build a relationship with them first. They need to understand you aren't going to harm them. I am often seen on my knees talking to the ladies; getting on your knees or sitting on the ground makes you less threatening to them. Use a soft gentle voice and make your movements slow and fluid. Bribes are also in order! They may not come to your hand immediately so scatter some scratch or mealworms around you so they can come close to you. A few days of this and you can advance slowly by putting treats in your hand, some will be brave enough to eat from your hand.

Eventually they will let you pet them. So, how do you pick them up? Slide one hand underneath them from front to back, put your other hand gently on her back. The hand that is under her needs to be able to hold her legs too, so slip your thumb and ring finger around her legs and gently hold them. With your second hand over her back lift her up, you have control of her feet and wings now and she will feel fairly secure with her chest resting on your forearm. Continue talking to her softly, she will possibly be tense and wary the first few times but will eventually relax. You can walk around with her like this, but many keepers prefer to tuck her under the arm facing behind, this way you have complete control and a free hand.

Holding a hen safely and securely is important for the safety and well- being of the hen and yourself. Beaks and claws can inflict some nasty wounds, so be gentle with the hens and they will be gentle with you! It is much easier to safely pick up hens that have been touched and held as chicks since they are used to the feeling and some even actively seek you out for petting and holding. Some breeds are definitely not 'touchy-feely' birds, so if you want to have hens that will be friendlier towards you research your breeds before you buy.

As an example, many of my birds are four to five years old and most tolerate being picked up, held and inspected without much fuss. The Marans however are convinced I'm going to murder them and can be quite a handful sometimes. They aren't stupid either, if I manage to catch one the others will keep their distance until bedtime. So if you have birds that are reluctant, wait until bedtime and then just pluck them off the roost, it's much easier and less stressful for everyone concerned.

Tip: Wait till bedtime and pick them up off the roost

Taming Chickens
Chickens are smart and they learn quickly and have good reasoning abilities. If you start them as chicks it's easier to bribe them to do things, but adult chickens can learn also. Social media has a lot of videos' showing pet chickens doing tricks for treats. A

tasty morsel will keep a chicken focused and interested for a long time but as with training any animal repetition is the key. If you just want them to be friendly towards you and follow you around the yard food is the answer. Once they associate you with food or treats, they are going to flock to you!

Chapter 10 Checklist

- Be able to identify a broody hen and know how to 'break' her
- Know how to protect your hens from predators and which security measures should be taken
- Know the appropriate measures to take during extreme weather conditions
- Be able to catch and safely handle your hens.

11 THE PECKING ORDER

We've all heard the phrase 'the pecking order'. In our minds eye, we likely see colleagues and co-workers neatly arranged in order of 'merit'. From the CEO down to the janitor, everyone has a place in the pecking order. The term pecking order was first coined in 1921 by Thorleif Schjelderup-Ebbe to describe the hierarchy of flock dynamics and it came into popular usage in the 1930s.

At times the pecking order can make life extremely difficult for both chickens and chicken keepers! In this chapter you will understand exactly what the pecking order is and how you can stop common problems caused because of the pecking order.

What is The Pecking Order

So, exactly what is it and how does it relate to you and your flock?

It's a system by which birds arrange their social standing in the flock. The higher ranked birds will get the best food, water and roosts while the lower placed birds will get the leftovers. This method of organization places each member of the flock on a hierarchy ladder. At the top of the ladder will be the head rooster (or hen if no rooster is present). This complex social order is designed to ensure that there is good cohesion between members, and few if any petty squabbles.

This sort of co-operation between members of the flock

ensures the survival of the flock by giving the best chances to the fittest birds. It is a flexible structure and within the flock there are usually three different types of social order going on:
• Rooster to Rooster
• Hens to Hens
• Roosters to Hens

A rooster may go up the ladder if he mounts a successful campaign against the leader. He becomes the new chicken-in-charge! And the defeated roosters go down the ladder, as do weak or sickly birds. Roosters that are lower in the order, crow less frequently and rarely mate.

Figure 12: A Rooster Preparing to Challenge the Pecking Order

Hens have their own 'girls' only ladder. The matriarchs of the flock will be up to the top of the ladder, with less dominant birds at the bottom. In this system the older, stronger and more savvy hens will be at the top. Young pullets just coming to point of lay, will try to move up the social ladder quickly. If a bird tries to go out of turn, she will earn glares, pecks and feather pulling from the higher 'ranked' hens. Usually a look or a quick peck is enough to remind the lower ranking hen she has overstepped the boundary.

The serious games of the pecking order start when chicks are around six weeks of age. Chicks will start rushing at each other, bumping chests and flaring feathers. These are all methods used to intimidate flock mates at any stage of life. By the time they leave the brooder, they will have their own pecking order sorted out.

Pecking Order Problems

Whilst the pecking order can create a sense of harmony within a flock it can also create absolute havoc, with chickens fighting each other for their position within the order. A full on pecking order assault is a violent and terrible thing to see. Older birds can be relentless, drawing blood, causing serious injury even death. There is nothing gentle about the pecking order.

Adding New Birds to Your Flock

Adding birds to your existing flock will cause a shift in the pecking order. The older birds will be very suspicious of the new members and can be quite violent about it. If you do add new birds to your flock, it needs to be done slowly and cautiously. You should never add less than two birds to an established flock.

The method that has worked well for me in the past is the separation pen. This is an area that the new hens can be put safely without the older girls being able to peck them. They can look, pace around the enclosure but can't get in. I do this for a week or so then open up the enclosure.

Figure 13: Chicken mesh used to and barricade off an area.

When you do open up the temporary enclosure you need to have places the new birds can hide or run to if flock members get really mean. I have not had any integration problems using this method- a couple of pecks here and there, but nothing too vicious. As a keeper, you should not intervene unless blood has been drawn, then you need to remove the injured bird quickly and isolate them. Remember to read Introducing New Chickens to Your Existing Flock for more help!

Sick or Injured Birds

Chickens rarely show any signs of illness or weakness. If they do, other flock members will pick on them and either drive them from the flock or kill them. This sounds awful, but remember, the flock in the wild is as strong as its' weakest member. It's simply a survival tactic.

If you have a chicken that is constantly being pecked at, you will need to isolate her away from harm. A large crate or 'chicken hospital' area will do very well. Check her over carefully for peck damage and also try to find out what is wrong with the bird.

The victim will need to be isolated until wounds are healed. Now comes the tough part, trying to re-integrate the affected bird. Use the segregation pen which we mentioned earlier on for a few days and then reintegrate her.

Bully Birds

Sometimes you have a hen who is a bully to everyone. Often she will be in the middle of the pecking order, rarely at the top. My bully bird is called Red Sonya and she is mid-level pecking order wise. When she sees a new girl anywhere near food she makes it her business to let them know they are not entitled to one beakful of food- it's hers! She dutifully 'patrols' the food stations for a day or so then loses interest. She has made her point and the newbies avoid her!

If you have a hen like this, the best way to 'straighten her out' is the segregation pen for a few days. The pecking order will change while she is in isolation, so when she gets re-introduced she will be a 'newbie' and treated accordingly. Once in a while you will get two or more hens that form a 'bully club'. Use the same treatment for them, except re-introduce them to the flock on separate days- this should break the pattern of bullying!

How to Avoid Pecking Order Problems

The good news is that much can be done by the keeper to ensure that old and new flock members integrate fairly peacefully.

First and most importantly, each bird needs to have sufficient 'personal space'. There really isn't a 'perfect formula' for space requirements, often quoted is four square foot/bird for floor space. If they are confined within the coop twenty four hours a day, I would certainly add as much room as possible, since boredom leads to mischief! If however, your birds are allowed to free range, coop space doesn't really become an issue until winter. I provide my girls with one foot of roosting space per bird. Mine all cram together on the roosts at night, leaving lots of empty roosting space! As you can see, it's very much an individual thing- some birds like space, others not so much.

Make sure you provide lots of roosting spots so that a hen can get away if she needs to. Providing places to 'hide' is important- old boxes, straw bales (outside the coop) dark quiet areas in the barn/shed. If you can think along the lines of a two year old playing hide and seek, you will have great success! Also, don't forget to provide extra feeding and watering stations. I usually provide four for a flock of thirty hens, this gives everyone a chance to eat and drink in peace.

Chapter 11 Checklist

• Understand exactly what the pecking order is
• Know the common problems caused by misbalanced pecking order
• Are able to take steps to correct pecking order problems

12 CHICKEN HEALTH ISSUES

Many of the ailments that can affect chickens are easily avoided by good housekeeping. Even if they do catch something it can usually be treated effectively when they are found early on in the course of the disease. A filthy coop is a breeding ground for flies and a host of microbes that cause disease. This chapter is designed as a guide to preventative measures and how to treat some of the simpler afflictions.

Biosecurity

Biosecurity has been brought to the forefront of our attention by the Avian Influenza outbreaks of 2015. The huge losses sustained by the poultry industry had most backyard keepers worried about their own flocks succumbing to this deadly disease.

What does biosecurity mean to you and your flock? It means taking appropriate care and precautionary measures to avoid introducing disease to your hens. Ideally you would have a closed flock, meaning all your birds come in at once and there are no more additions except for flock hatchlings. In practice this rarely happens except for commercial flocks. However, there are several precautions that you can take to prevent disease from attacking your flock.

Quarantine

Any and all new birds you get must be quarantined for a minimum of two weeks, preferably four weeks. They should be separate from your main flock, preferably in another area where they can't breathe in the same air. Many diseases are spread by coughs and sneezes, so they should remain a good distance from your flock and where your flock can't visit with them.

Tip: If you have show birds, they too should be quarantined from the rest of the flock, they may have been exposed to any number of diseases while in the show arena.

Cleanliness and Sanitation

This means keeping coops clean, removing poop frequently, changing bedding often and cleaning drinkers and feeders regularly. It also entails keeping a check on the rodent population that inevitably arrives where there is food available. Rodents really don't care what they walk on and their feet are often sources of contamination. They will also urinate and poop in feed sacks and waterers. Aggressive management may be needed if there are lots of them. Any sighting of them during the day time is a good indicator that you have a serious problem on your hands.

Keeping weeds and grass down around the coop area will also help to prevent rodents from visiting the coop unseen. Clean up the area each night so there are no food remnants to attract wildlife and remove drinkers from the area too. Wild birds can spread disease also, so make sure your bird feeders are well away from the coop area.

Flies are another nuisance pest that can spread disease, keeping the poop piles under control will limit the amount of flies you will get. You can also hang fly papers if you have sufficient headroom in your coop, but make sure your birds cannot get tangled up in it.

Traffic Control

This means keeping visitors to your flock minimal and at a distance. Don't let other keepers into your chicken yard unless they are wearing boot covers or have stepped into a disinfectant footbath. Your clothing and shoes can also bring in disease (ideally you will have one pair of boots dedicated to livestock chores). If you have been anywhere with poultry other than your own, you should always change clothing before you tend to your flock. It may seem a bit over the top, but prevention is the best practice.

Parasites in the Coop

Parasites are generally divided into internal such as round worms or external such as lice. Below we will give you a rundown on both types and treatment for them. They are by far the most prevalent disease among chickens.

Internal

Worms come in several forms: tape, round, gape and eye. Tape and round worm inhabit the intestinal tract of chickens. A bad infestation of either can cause watery diarrhea, dehydration, depressed appetite and decreased egg-laying. The bird will often be seen sitting alone. These worms can be easily treated by using Wazine. If you are unsure whether your birds have worms or not, take a poop sample to the vet for testing.

Gape worms inhabit the respiratory tract, if the infection is severe the bird will 'gape' its mouth to breath; hence the name. Mild infections can be treated with Wazine, but severe infection will require a veterinary consult for treatment.

An organism that can be found anywhere there is a chicken is coccidia. This nasty little protozoa can cause coccidiosis in chicks under the right circumstances. It is a devastating disease causing high mortality in those affected and if a chick survives coccidiosis she will likely not be a good producer of eggs. Coccidiosis can be treated with Corid if found early enough. Chicks can be vaccinated at Day 1 by hatcheries. It should be noted that coccidia are present in all chickens, it's only when they get out of control, that they cause disease.

Tip: When using Wazine, or other medicine in chickens, most have a 'withdrawal' period. This is the amount of time that the eggs are not considered safe to eat. The period is usually between seven and fourteen days.

External

Lice, fleas, bed bugs and mites all will enjoy a tasty meal on a chicken. When you perform your monthly health checks, take a good look around the vent, under wings and just at the tail feather base. Ruffle through the feathers down to the skin, and if you have 'critters' you need to dust. Chicken fleas are chicken specific, so you will not become infected! The good news is that they can all be treated with 'poultry dust', the trick is getting it on the chicken. Whatever method you use to treat be sure to dust well around the vent and tail feathers, under wings and on the abdomen. Try to avoid getting the dust in their eyes or near the face since it will be an irritant to the lungs. Treatment will need to be repeated in seven to ten days. The roosts and coop should be treated also with the dust.

Scaly Leg Mite

The burrowing mite that causes this is knemidokoptes mutans. It burrows under the scales of the leg causing them to lift up as the mite leaves detritus behind it. It is painful and irritating for the afflicted bird and is contagious to your flock. As you run your fingers up the birds leg normally it will be a little 'textured', with mites the edges are most definitely raised. Treatment consists of soaking the feet and legs in warm water, gently removing any dirt from the area. Take the bird out of the water and dry the legs and feet well. Next apply Neem oil with a toothbrush making sure you are getting the oil underneath the scales, when you have done this slather olive oil on the legs. Repeat every three days until the problem is gone. Unfortunately it can take months to fully treat.

Tip: Some home remedies call for the use of motor oil, kerosene or gasoline applied to the legs. These items are toxic and should not be used.

Providing your flock with a dust bathing area will help to keep infestations minimal. You can use a combination of wood ash and peat moss in a large bin or basin. The hens will use it often so you will need to top it off frequently.

Please bear caution with medications though. More and more chicken keepers are using medicine like Ivermectin and Frontline to treat infestations. These medicines are not licensed for use in chickens, so you really should consult a veterinarian about 'off label' usage of any drug. I only treat my birds when I see evidence of infestation, preferring to not overuse medications. Some folks treat their birds regularly at six monthly intervals. There is no right or wrong it is simply personal preference.

Tip: If your chickens are reluctant to go to bed at night, check the roosts carefully with a flashlight. If you spot grey 'dust' you have mites in the coop. The chickens don't want to go to bed and be bitten by these pests.

Flystrike
This happens infrequently, but can be deadly if not treated. Flystrike happens when you have a hen with poopy feathers around the vent. A fly will lay eggs and when the maggots hatch they will eat the poop and feathers. When they run out of poop, they will start to eat the healthy flesh off the hen. For a mild case you can soak the hen in a warm bath, then towel her off. You will have to remove the maggots one by one. If you aren't up to this find a friend or relative that will help or go see the vet. The successful treating of this may take several days, even weeks in severe cases. The wounds will be treated with antibiotic cream or powder.

Health Checks

Every day that you see your flock, you should be taking mental notes on their demeanor. Is Elsie quiet today? Mildred has gone broody etc., you probably do it without thinking. If your flock is small then you can keep this information in your head, but when you have a larger flock what to do? I use a monthly check sheet to keep track of my flock. A check sheet doesn't have to be complicated, it can cover the basics and no more.

Each month you should check the following on your birds:
- Eyes: Should be bright and clear
- Comb and wattles: Should be red and intact (there are some breed exceptions to this)
- Crop: Should be full, not pendulous or empty
- Feathers: Glossy, shiny and tight
- Legs/feet: Shanks should be smooth with no raised scales, feet should show no evidence of bumblefoot or other issues
- Vent: Clean, moist and pink
- Activity: Should be active, if she's sitting alone and is hunched up then something is wrong

You can add in other notes such as age, how many chicks a broody hatched and so on. I find that having a written record helps me to pinpoint any problems in my flock.

If you have birds that are reluctant to be picked up and inspected, wait until they are on the roost, then pluck off the one you want to check over. The hen will be sleepy and will not create too much fuss and will be easier to handle.

Tip: If you have several hens of the same breed and can't tell who you have checked and who needs to be checked, consider using leg bands to differentiate between birds.

Common Chicken Diseases

These are the most common problems that backyard keepers are likely to see in their flock at some point.

Bumblefoot
We mentioned this earlier in our health check list. Bumblefoot is caused by the bacteria Staph. Aureus. Its' point of entry is usually a miniscule cut to the foot pad or a splinter. The wound will heal, but a 'bumble' will grow. It is a black, usually circular patch of skin which can be on the foot pad or between the toes. When noticed early it can be treated with antibiotics, occasionally it may need to be surgically removed. If left untreated, it can cause system wide infection from which the hen will die.

Vent Prolapse
This is an emergency! It arises from one of the following:
• Too large an egg which makes the hen strain to expel it
• Young pullets made to lay too soon
• Older, fat hens
• Calcium deficiency

The good news is it is treatable, but the bad news is it is likely to happen again. Prolapsed vent is quite easy to spot, the vent turns itself inside out so there is a red, glistening protrusion at the back end. You will need to isolate this hen immediately since her sisters will peck at it causing further damage. You will need to clean all the tissue well with a mild antiseptic solution or plain soap and warm water. Apply a hemorrhoid cream to the vent inside and out, then with your gloved finger, gently insert the vent back into the hen. It may pop out a couple of times, but keep on re-inserting using the above sequence each time.

The hen needs to stay quiet for a few days, so put her in a dimly lit area to discourage her from laying. She will need to be given extra vitamin, calcium and electrolytes in her water. Once she has healed, you can re-introduce her to the flock slowly. Keep a close watch on her, as prolapsed vent has a tendency to reoccur.

Egg Yolk Peritonitis
Egg yolk peritonitis happens when the yolk is released from the

ovary into the body cavity instead of the infundibulum (oviduct). The yolk is an almost perfect medium for bacteria to set up shop in. The bacteria in question can be E. Coli, salmonella or pasteurella. As we already mentioned, hens are very good at hiding the fact they are ill, so by the time you have usually noted the symptoms the hen is extremely ill. Symptoms include pale comb/wattles; dull eyes; reluctant to move; sitting alone; looks disheveled and swollen abdomen. If your hen exhibits any of these symptoms she should be taken to the vet as soon as possible, peritonitis is an emergency. The treatment is antibiotics, but unfortunately this problem has a very high mortality rate.

Egg Bound

If your hen is walking like a penguin or you are seeing her pumping her tail up and down, she is trying to expel an egg. To confirm your suspicions you can gently insert your gloved and lubed index finger into her vent. You need to go straight back for about one to two inches very gently. You may be able to feel the egg, if you do apply more lubrication inside the vent. Then soak her abdomen in warm water and Epsom salts for twenty minutes or so, gently massaging her belly at the same time. Remove her from the tub, gently towel her off and apply a hemorrhoidal cream to the vent area. Place her in a quiet, darkened safe place and check on her in an hour to see if she has passed the egg. If she hasn't try the soaking tub again, you may need to repeat this a few times. If after three times she doesn't pass the egg, she will need taking to the local veterinarian.

Mareks Disease

Mareks disease is caused by a herpes virus and is quite widespread over the continent. It will depend on the particular strain that your bird may catch as to presentation of symptoms. The severity of the virus can be non-apparent (no symptoms) to the disturbing sight of the neurological presentation. In its most dramatic presentation the bird will seemingly do the splits, be unable to weight bear, its head may twist back and it will suffer severe respiratory distress. There is no cure for Mareks disease yet. The vaccine does not confer immunity; it will only make the symptoms lessen in severity.

Mareks has a few different presentations, one of which is the internal growth of tumors. These tumors are only noticed post mortem. Many flocks are infected with Mareks and yet show no symptoms at all and the birds live out their life in full. Mareks disease should not be seen as a 'death sentence' to your flock, as some flock members may succumb to it while others will not be affected. The survivors will be carriers for the rest of their days.

Frostbite

Frostbite occurs when damp cold air freezes the extremities of an animal. In chickens it is usually the comb, wattles and feet. This is one reason that good ventilation is essential in the coop. Chickens can tolerate cold much better than humans as they have lots of feathers to keep them warm. When there is moisture in the air, it will form condensation on exposed surfaces. Roosters are always prime candidates for frozen combs and wattles, as are breeds with large combs such as Leghorns.

Preventative measures include adequate ventilation, reduction of drafts blowing on the birds, placing wider perches so they can cover their feet with the feathers and using Vaseline or similar on combs and wattles to form a barrier between the air and skin.

Summary

Resistance to disease is controlled by several factors such as nutrition, age, environment and wellbeing. A young healthy chicken is likely to shake off a case of the sniffles while an older hen might not. Resistance to some diseases can be conferred by vaccination such as coccidiosis, salmonella and Mareks. If you buy birds from a hatchery it is worthwhile checking to see if they can be vaccinated prior to shipping.

Chickens are extremely good at hiding problems from you. In the wild, a sick or slow chicken would not be tolerated in the flock as it would be a target for predators, so chickens became good at hiding illness or infirmity from everyone. If you are keeping health journals for your flock, you may be able to pick up on subtle clues, but most likely the problem will be severe before it comes to your notice or you will find a dead hen.

These are the most common problems in backyard flocks. It's important to remember that there are some diseases out there that are a significant threat to not only your flock but other local poultry owners. Diseases such as exotic Newcastle Disease and Avian Influenza need to be reported to the USDA/APHIS. These diseases are so contagious, that all flock members will be culled in order to prevent the spread of the disease. Fortunately, outbreaks of these diseases are very sporadic, so you are unlikely to be affected.

If you do have a bird die from an unknown cause and you have other sick birds, you can report the death and save the body for a post mortem by the USDA/APHIS veterinary specialist. These autopsies are usually done free or for a nominal fee.

Chapter 12 Checklist

- Have a good understanding of biosecurity
- Plan your health checks and their frequency
- Know which are the most common chicken diseases and parasites and how to treat them

13 WHY YOUR CHICKENS STOPPED LAYING EGGS

It's always a cause for concern when your chickens stop laying. In fact, noticing this can help you identify if your chickens are ill. That's why we always keep track of the amount of eggs our chickens lay - this way we know straight away if somethings wrong.

There are lots of reasons why your chickens might have stopped laying, but you don't need to rush out and buy super market eggs just yet! In this chapter we are going to look at the most common reasons why your chickens have stopped laying and what you can do to get them laying again.

Their Diet

The most common reason why your chickens have stopped laying is there is something wrong with their diet. Have you recently changed their diet or even changed the brand of pellets which you are feeding your chickens? We once decided to stop feeding our chickens layers pellets and to start feeding them maize instead. When feeding the girls layers pellets we were getting a minimum of 9 eggs a day and after feeding them Maize for a matter of days we were only getting 4-5 eggs a day!

Tip: This was because maize doesn't contain much protein and chickens need around 20 grams of protein each day to continue laying eggs.

Just remember whatever you are feeding your chickens they need a proper balanced diet to ensure their bodies are capable of producing eggs. If you are feeding your girls layers pellets and they are still struggling to lay, consider giving them snacks which are high in protein such as: pumpkin seeds, oats or mealworms. Another often neglected aspect of their diet is water. If chickens don't have access to fresh water all day round you can say goodbye to your eggs.

Not Enough Daylight

So you've made sure your girls are getting plenty of protein and fresh water, but there are still no eggs in sight. Sometimes it can just be the wrong time of the year for your hens to lay. To lay eggs your chickens need plenty of natural daylight, at least 14 hours a day; 16 hours is even better. This means that during the winter, when in the US, the natural daylight can drop to less than 9 hours a day; your girls would need 5 more hours of daylight to lay eggs. The solution to this is to place an artificial light in their coop and set this on an automated timer. This will certainly keep your egg production high but it's something we would never do.

There's a reason why hens don't lay as much during the winter... their body needs to rest and recover for the next year. And if you don't give them time for their bodies to recover you will do more harm than good in the long run. It's not all bad news though, your hens shouldn't stop laying completely and you should get the occasional egg, but that's about it.

Broody Hens

So your girls are well fed, getting plenty of sunlight, but they still aren't laying. It's time to give up on them and get a new flock... only joking! You might have a broody hen and in this case she won't lay eggs no matter how much protein or sunshine you give her. When a hen gets broody she wants to hatch her own chicks, so she will sit on top of her eggs for 21 days until they hatch. During this 21 day period she won't lay any eggs.

Figure 14: Broody Hen Laying on Eggs

There are obvious signs to look out for if your hen is broody:
• She will sit in the nest box all day.
• She will become very territorial and stop anything getting near her eggs.
• She will remove her breast feathers to give the eggs heat from her body.

Tip: If you think your hen is broody, read how to stop my broody hen in Chapter 10.

New Additions to the Flock

So you've definitely not got a broody hen, but still don't see any eggs. Have you recently moved your chickens or introduced new chickens into the flock? Chickens love routine and the slightest disruption to their routine usually results in them going off lay. The most common routine disruption they experience is when they are moved. This can either be when they are transported to your home after you've purchased them, or if you've decided to move their coop. Chances are you bought your chickens as pullets so they weren't laying when they arrived anyway. But if you've moved their coop they will not be happy with you! Give them a few days to come around and they should start laying again.

If you've just introduced new chickens into the flock this can also disrupt their routine and egg laying. When new chickens are introduced there tends to be some shoving and jostling for the first few days as they establish the new pecking order. During this time they won't lay eggs, but again, after a few days they should start laying again.

Certain breeds just don't lay as well as others and we sometimes forget this, especially when we read about how great other people's eggs are. Breeds such as Rhode Island Reds or Buff Orpingtons can lay more than 200 eggs per year. Whereas other breeds such as Ameraucanas or Silkies are known to lay less than 100 eggs a year.

If you're unsure about how many eggs a year your breed of chicken should lay, this beginner's guide to chicken breeds in Chapter 2 should help.

Old Age

So you've got a Rhode Island Red, which should be laying over 200 eggs a year, and they have just stopped laying. Unfortunately as chickens get older the amount of eggs they lay slows down. Look at the image below and you can see you normally only get around 3 years of good egg laying from a chicken.

If your Rhode Island Red laid 200 eggs in their first year, they should lay around 170 eggs in their second year and 130 eggs in their third year. This number will continue to decrease down to around 40 eggs by their tenth year.

If your chickens are getting slightly older then a decrease in their egg laying is perfectly natural and expected. There is nothing you can do about this and it is simply nature's way as your chickens age.

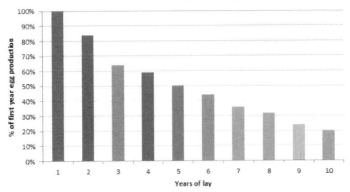

Illness

If you have a settled, young chicken, that is well fed, has plenty of natural daylight and they have suddenly stopped laying chances are that they are ill.

Colds

Symptoms to look out for include slimy nostrils and them walking around with their beak open because they can't breathe through their nose. Make sure to isolate any chicken which you think might have a cold to stop it spreading to the rest of the flock.

Parasites

This includes lice, mites and worms. You will notice your chickens comb will go pale and they won't stop itching themselves. The easiest way to treat any parasite is to spray both the chicken coop and the chickens with poultry cleaner. Something like Johnsons Poultry Housing spray should do the trick.

Molts

Many people confuse the symptoms above as an illness when actually the chicken is molting. Chickens molt each year and it can take around 6 to 12 weeks for them to grow back new feathers-during this time period they will not lay eggs.

Tip: Make sure to read Chapter 12 for common health issues.

Chapter 13 Checklist

- Importance of protein in their diets
- Know that change in their routine alters their egg laying
- Know how old age impacts egg laying
- Appreciate that egg laying is a good indicator of a hen's health

14 SEVEN OF THE BIGGEST CHICKEN MYTHS

Sometimes old wives tales linger on long enough to become folk legends that people still believe in to this day. As people become more and more disconnected from their food source, the 'legends' continue and can even expand. Over the years I've heard many myths about chickens, some entertaining, but others just outright lies!

In this chapter we are going to straighten out some of those for you in this lighthearted, but critical look at chicken myths.

Chickens Can't Lay Eggs without Roosters

I have lost count of the number of people that have asked this question! My answer is to give them a lesson in human reproductive biology; a woman can ovulate without a man, but needs the man only if she wants a baby: it is basically the same for a hen. A chicken will ovulate once about every twenty five hours. Thus, an egg will be laid slightly later every day until she 'misses' a day.

The rooster sperm has a long journey ahead of it since the egg will be fertilized before the shell is laid down. A hen can store sperm from the rooster for about two weeks in little pockets in the reproductive system. The eggs a hen lays without being fertilized are perfectly fine to eat, as are fertilized eggs. In some cultures, a delicacy called 'balat' is eaten. This is an egg with a chick embryo formed inside the shell- although I have seen balat, I would never eat it.

Many folks will tell you a rooster is needed not only for the eggs, but also to keep order in the flock. This is not so. A dominant female hen will take the lead in a flock and underlings will follow her. Although they may not range quite as far without the protection of a rooster, they still forage.

Chickens are Stupid

Far from it! Of course, like people, there are some smarter than others but in general, chickens are intelligent, thinking creatures. Research done over several years, indicate that chickens are much more than just 'nuggets in waiting'. They have a complex social structure called the pecking order. The phrase doesn't really convey the depth of the relationships between one chicken and the next, but each bird in the flock knows its place in relationship to every other bird of the same flock and they compare themselves against other!

They have over thirty different sounds ranging from 'I've laid an egg' to 'danger! Hide quickly'. They are capable of recognizing up to one hundred individuals, including humans and retaining those memories for future use.

They are able to solve some fairly complex problems such as basic arithmetic and self-control! They can be creative and flexible which can help them to solve new problems in novel ways, even chicks have been shown to be able to navigate by using very basic geometry.

They are as smart as a toddler and can grasp some things that toddlers only figure out later in their life. As an example, if you show a three year old something and then hide it, the toddler will lose interest and forget about it- not chickens! They understand that the thing still exists although hidden from view.

The more socially dominant birds are usually the ones who lead and teach the flock. An example would be the head rooster leading the flock to a new food source or fresh water. Chickens have also been shown to have empathy and can form inter-species bonds, such as with their flock keeper. I'm not sure if grieving is the right word here, but when one of my dominant females died recently, almost every other chicken came and stood by her for a moment or two.

Chickens are Vegetarian

Chickens are actually omnivorous and will eat just about anything they care to. I have watched in horrified fascination as my gentle girls dismember and eat frogs, mice and baby snakes. Once the flock notices that someone has a tasty morsel the chase is on and it becomes a tug o' war to get a piece of the food.

In general, they eat mainly feed stuff, weeds, insects, seeds, leftovers and of course, the treats we give them. If you have ever sat and watched your flock patrolling the yard, you will have seen them picking at the grass and weeds, scratching through the dirt to get some grit, chasing butterflies is also a favorite pastime! The compost heap is a favorite restaurant for my girls, bugs, worms and left-overs are all fine chicken cuisine. They benefit by getting tasty little morsels and I benefit from the girls turning the heap on a daily basis.

As we know, most of their nutritional requirements come from the pellet or crumble feed that we give them, although hens that are allowed out to pasture have eggs that are phenomenally full of goodness. So as you see not so much the vegetarian chick!

Roosters are Mean

Well I have to admit, there is some truth in this, but it only applies to some roosters. As a chick, roosters are as adorable as the girls, but when they reach adolescence hormones start to transform them.

It is important to realize he is not specifically targeting you. His little rooster brain is setting him up for domination over the hens. This role also entails protecting them from threats (possibly you), finding food and water for them and populating the world with his offspring. Many roosters will try to 'flog' you at least once. Flogging is when they fly at you and beat you with their wings-usually the claws are not involved in this test of boundaries.

Tip: The key to establishing roles is to not tolerate flogging from day one. Some people think it's cute and don't think it's a problem until it's too late.

If the rooster believes it's ok to do this, he will keep testing his boundaries. A rooster can give you a nasty peck or gash from the talons. If a rooster is treated firmly he will respect you and take care of his hens without seeing you as a threat. There are many ways to keep a rooster in his place; it seems everyone has a favorite trick or two.

My personal preference now is to carry something long enough to prod him with, from a distance and thin enough to give a reminder without hurting him. It seems to be working for my current roosters. Some roosters are very mellow and never have to be shown who is boss. Then there are others that no matter what you do, they are mean.

Chickens are Dirty and Smelly

A chicken coop is as clean as the keeper maintains it. Yes the poop can be a bit ripe at times, but if you clean the poop trays regularly, this is not a problem. In the heat of summer, poop attracts flies and other nasty bugs, so please try to remove it at least every other day.

An unsanitary coop can lead to 'flystrike'. This is where the fly will lay eggs on the mucky rear end of a bird. When the maggots hatch, they will eat all the filth but then start on the healthy flesh of the hen. Also in summer, the fumes from the poop's ammonia become more pungent and can affect the respiratory and eye health of your hens.

Shop Bought Eggs are the Same

Whoever said this plainly did not know the truth! The visual difference between store bought and freshly laid is easy to see. In general, a store egg yolk will be much paler than the beautiful golden yolk you get from your own hen. Also, store eggs spread over the pan when cracked- why? It's because they are not fresh. A fresh egg when cracked with hold together well.

Nutritionally the pastured egg wins the prize for being the perfect food! There have been scientific studies that have investigated store bought eggs versus pastured eggs. The pastured eggs ran off with the prize as they contain twice as much omega 3 fatty acids and vitamin A, three times as much vitamin E, seven times beta carotene and four times vitamin D. They are also significantly lower in cholesterol and saturated fats!

Tip: Chickens that are given flax seed in addition to their diet will produce eggs that are omega 3 enriched.

Generally speaking, the lower the cost of an egg, the lower the nutritional value will be just because the hens are kept in poorer conditions. If you still buy eggs you can visit the Cornucopia Institute's website as they maintain a scorecard that rates various egg producers around the country.

Chickens Carry Disease

It's a fact that every living thing has its own unique flora of bacteria. Everyone that you see each day, talk with regularly and work with, even you, are populated by unique blends of bacteria. This goes for animals too: dogs, cats, goldfish and yes, chickens! Our personal 'brand' of bacteria does not cause us any trouble, we have a symbiotic relationship. The problems only start to arise when bacteria from one animal invades another. This is known as a zoonotic disease, meaning it can travel between species.

It seems we read almost daily about people getting sick with salmonella, listeria or E. Coli. While it's true that you can get these diseases from backyard chickens, it is highly unlikely if you use good hygiene such as hand washing. Recently, smaller, very limited outbreaks in several areas of the country have been traced to improper hygiene used in handling homestead chickens. If you butcher your own birds it is essential that it be done cleanly and carefully, otherwise the possibility of salmonella or E. Coli can become very real.

As much as you may enjoy cuddling with your birds, please do not kiss them! You run a much higher risk of contracting disease if you are putting your lips on the bird- it's also possible for the bird to catch something from you!

Chapter 14 Checklist

• Know which of the popular urban legends about chickens are true
• Tell the difference between shop bought and freshly laid eggs

15 TOP 10 WAYS TO ACCIDENTALLY KILL YOUR CHICKENS

Over recent years, many people have taken the plunge and decide to keep chickens. Unfortunately, some people have done so without even doing basic research into the care and upkeep of their flock. Subsequently, some birds languish or die simply from lack of appropriate care or attention. Fortunately you don't fall into this group of people because you are taking the time to research how to care for chickens.

In this chapter we discuss the most common ways in which chicks or chickens health and survival can be severely impacted and what you can do to avoid these things.

Coop Fires

This is the number one cause of death for many chicks. Setting up the heat lamp safely is very important, not only for the safety of your birds, but your property too. The number of coop or barn fires caused by heat lamps that have not been secured correctly is depressing.

In springtime people get ready for the chicks by preparing the brooder, bedding etc. and of course, a heat lamp. Heat of some type is needed to keep the chicks warm through their first few weeks of life. I cannot stress enough to double and triple check the securing of the heat lamp. If the lamp should fall into the bedding, it will start a fire in less than two minutes as the heat from the lamp is that intense.

I have recently used a heating plate for my chicks with great success and little fear of fire. I do, however, use a heat lamp on occasion. I use a metal chain to suspend the fixture, duct tape to secure the wiring and an extra securing with strong twine for safety!!

Tip: Adult chickens do not need extra heat over the winter. They are able to keep themselves warm enough, adding a lamp is not necessary.

Family Pets

Dogs love to chase things, rabbits, cats, the mailman, and baby chicks. It is their nature to do this and expecting them to not chase chicks is a bit optimistic. Dogs can be trained to interact with chickens, but it takes time and patience on everyone's behalf.

Many folks have dogs and cats happily co-existing with their flock. Training a puppy is best since they can be trained easily at this age. An older dog can learn but the process will be longer and many folks do not have the time or patience for correction training. If you simply don't have the time, ensure that your chickens are safe from your dog(s). Be aware that smaller terrier type dogs will dig under wire, so you need to protect against that possibility by burying your wire mesh.

Lack of Security

Chicken is a favorite dinner for many predators including foxes, raccoons, hawks and so forth, so you need to have top notch security for your birds. Your coop should be able to withstand assault from many different sources. Rats for instance will gnaw through the base or side of a run to access the feed, eggs or small chicks. Always check your coop perimeters weekly for signs of damage.

Tip: A good way to ensure that rats don't eat through the floor of the coop is to cover it with half inch hardware cloth. This prevents them from gaining access to your flock.

We all know how cute raccoons are right? You won't think so if one gets into your coop. They are incredibly smart and can figure out how to open simple locks. It has been said that if a three year old child can open a lock, so can a raccoon. Use locking mechanisms that require an opposable thumb to open- raccoons can't open these.

Hawks are difficult to protect against if you pasture your chickens. Birds of prey are protected species so cannot be trapped or harmed. If you have an outside run, try to cover it over with wire mesh (chicken wire will do here). If that isn't possible, string a thick twine, or something similar, across the top of the run in a random fashion. The idea is to disrupt the flight path of the bird and make it extremely difficult to enter and leave the run from above.

Tip: Chicken wire keeps chickens in, but will not keep predators out! Many people have found this out the hard way thinking their birds are secure and safe only to find it wasn't so.

Poison

It is said that if you have poultry you will have vermin. Rats, mice, voles and chipmunks will all visit the henhouse looking for food. There are several ways to deter these visitors and one of them is the use of poison. Bait stations can be enclosed so that chickens cannot reach the poison itself, but the rodent will leave the station and go to die somewhere else. If the carcass is found by the chickens they will peck at it and possibly eat it- they can become very ill or simply die themselves.

• There are three different types of poison in common use:

• Bromethalin: This is a very potent neurotoxin that kills within twenty four hours. This type of poison has no antidote, so should not be used around livestock, pets or small children.

• Vitamin Based: Will kill within twenty four hours. This does have an antidote but should be used cautiously when animals, birds and small children are present.

• Anti-Coagulants: Probably the most widely used poison around. It is slow acting so takes time to be effective. Again, this needs to be used cautiously around livestock. If you suspect an animal has ingested any of these, call the veterinarian immediately.

Always use poison with extreme caution around any livestock, pets and children. Animals can and do eat poisoned meat and become sick themselves.

Chickens and Chemicals Don't Mix

If you house your chickens in a barn or some other multi-purpose building, make sure any chemicals are safely stored away. Chickens are plain nosey and will investigate just about anything if they think its food! Bleach, gasoline, oils, antifreeze should all be contained within a cupboard or placed out of reach for your hens. Livestock medicines are potentially deadly to hens if they can access an open container. They are incredibly curious creatures and will investigate almost anything, so be sure to close all containers tightly.

Figure 15: I told you chickens were curious

Glass, Wire and Nails

Whilst they are pecking around for grit and tidbits they may pick up small pieces of glass, wire, nails or other metal odds. The item is likely to lodge in the gizzard where it can cause bleeding, infection or even death. If you are working on a project make sure you clean up all your stuff. Have a small container on hand for any detritus to go into so the hens can't eat them!

Dehydration

In the summer heat, each hen can drink around a pint of water a day. They absolutely must have access to clean, fresh water at all times. I use three separate one gallon drinkers for thirty hens and I fill these daily at least once. If you are unable to check on the status of your drinkers frequently, simply buy bigger drinkers. It's quite easy to figure out how much water they will need; one hen = one pint. It is important to have more than one drinking station. Occasionally you will get a hen that will guard her drinker so the lowest in the pecking order may get deprived. Dehydration can quickly overcome a hen, eventually leading to death. If a hen has not had consistent access to water through the day, she will not lay eggs well for the next couple of weeks.

Neglect

If you are reading this, you are unlikely to be neglecting your birds! There are people who expect their hens to be completely self- sufficient and do not buy any feed believing that the chicken can find enough to live on in the yard. Certainly in earlier times this was the norm for chickens. They would scratch around on the farm and gather enough substance to stay alive. It should also be noted that in the 'old time' hens laid considerably fewer eggs because their diet was so bad.

Chickens can also be 'hoarded' just like cats and dogs. In these instances usually animal rescue services get involved. In fact, many bird rescue places will try to rehome hens with responsible owners.

Garden Plants

We all love to let out girls out to patrol the yard and dispatch unwelcome guests such as caterpillars and bugs. Are your garden plants safe for them to nibble at? I think most people know that foxglove gives us digitalis, a potent medicine that lowers the heart rate. It is most definitely not for chicken consumption! Some of the other toxic plants on the list are: holly, lobelia angels' trumpet, jimsonweed, pokeberry, sweet pea, honeysuckle, bleeding hearts, myrtle and elderberry.

This is by no means a comprehensive list these are just a few of the many toxic plants out there. Interestingly, many of those plants mentioned are also poisonous to humans too! Chickens are pretty smart (mostly) and avoid things they should not eat.

Lack of Health Care/Checks

We all know chickens need regular health checks. They can suffer from a variety of pests and parasites, so it is up to the responsible keeper to do regular checks on each bird. Parasites such as mites can make a bird become so anemic that the bird will die. A worm infestation can cause birds to drop weight, become lethargic and non-productive- gapeworm can even cause a bird to suffocate!

Every day when you see your girls, you should be making mental notes. Emily seems depressed today, Betty is preening excessively etc. Each of these mental notes will guide you when you check your hen over. Sometimes there isn't anything obvious wrong, but you get the feeling something is 'up'. This is being in tune with your flock and catching problems before they get out of hand. To ignore subtle warning signs are not a good policy and can be detrimental to the wellbeing of your entire flock.

16 FREQUENTLY ASKED QUESTIONS

Q: Do I need a rooster for eggs?
No, you don't need a rooster to have eggs. A hen will lay without any help from a rooster. If you want to raise chicks then you will need a rooster to fertilize the eggs.

Q: Can I raise chickens in the city?
The answer to this depends on where you live. Some cities allow chickens; usually a limited number of hens and no roosters. You will need to contact your local Zoning Officer. Also get yourself a copy of the zoning laws just to be sure; sometimes the law can fall to individual perception.

Q: Are chickens vegetarian?
Emphatically: NO! They will eat bugs, small snakes, mice, frogs and anything else that is too slow to get out of their way. Don't pay extra for feed that is advertised as 'vegetarian' since most feeds are vegetarian anyway.

Q: Can I eat fertilized eggs?
Yes you can, providing the eggs are fresh. If a fertilized egg is of indeterminate age, crack into a cup to make sure you don't have an embryo in there.

Q: My hens' feathers are falling out, why?
Is she old enough to molt? If she is over fifteen months she may be molting. Alternatively, her sisters may be pulling her

feathers out. Watch their behaviors, and if they are feather plucking, offer more calcium to them. Useful Chapters:

• Chapter 1: Do they have enough space?

Q: My hen won't get off the nest and pecks me when I try to move her.

She sounds like she is broody. If you want chicks, let her sit, if not or the eggs are unfertilized, take her off the nest (wear thick, protective gloves). You will likely have to do this several times in order to deter her.

Q: My hen laid a teeny, tiny egg, what's up?

New layers and occasionally older hens will lay a 'fairy' egg. It is an infrequent occurrence and not significant, a hiccup in the egg machinery. Remember that bantams lay smaller eggs than large breeds.

Q: I have an egg that's wrinkly and odd shaped, is it ok to eat?

This is a minor problem in the egg laying department, nothing to worry about. Yes, you can eat it.

Q: There is blood in my chickens' poop!

Chickens shed the lining of their intestine occasionally. If she is otherwise well and shows no signs of illness, just watch her. If it continues or she looks ill, you will need to seek veterinary advice.

Q: My hens are laying soft shelled eggs.

If they are laying soft or no shell eggs, they need a calcium supplement like oyster shell. Do not add it to their feed, just offer it in a separate feeder and they will eat what they need.

Q: My young pullet is squatting down every time I approach her, what's wrong?

Nothing is wrong, she is coming of age. This is a good sign that she is getting ready to lay eggs and breed. You should have eggs soon!

Q: My hen is eighteen weeks old and hasn't laid yet, is she sick?

What breed of bird is she? Some breeds such as Barbu D'Uccle and Orpingtons, won't lay until twenty four weeks or even more.

Useful Chapters:
- Chapter 8: Laying-Hen Management
- Chapter 10: Common Problems

Q: My hens are almost bald from an amorous rooster, what can I do?

If you want your hens to mate, buy (or make) them a chicken saddle. This covers their backs and protects them from his talons. If you don't want them to mate, I suggest you either build a 'bachelor pad' for him or remove him from the flock.

Q: A friend feeds her chickens scratch all the time instead of feed, is this ok?

No. The chickens are not getting the correct nutrition their bodies need. Scratch should be a supplement to their feed, not the main course. Useful Chapters:
- Chapter 7: Feed and Water

Q: My hens have suddenly stopped laying, why?

Hens' egg laying machinery is very sensitive and the smallest change can stop them laying. Have you recently changed their bedding or added a new chicken to the flock? Is the winter coming and reducing the amount of daylight hours? Useful Chapters:
- Chapter 13: Why Your Chickens Stopped Laying Eggs

Q: I have a bully hen and she picks on the smaller ones, what can I do?

First, do you have enough room for the little ones to escape from her? Insufficient space is probably the number one cause of anti-social behaviors. You can try putting out another feeder and drinker for the others to use. If none of this works, put her in a cage by herself for a couple of days, then re-introduce her. Useful Chapters:
- Chapter 9: How to Introduce New Chickens to Your Existing Flock

Q: How often should I clean feeders and drinkers and what should I use?

Feeders and drinkers should be cleaned weekly and during the hot months every couple of days. You can use bleach and water

1:10 ratio or you can use vinegar and water 1:1 ratio.

Q: My hen has something crawling in her feathers, what is it?

It sounds like chicken lice- don't panic! Use a poultry approved insecticidal dust and apply to your hen, paying special attention to the vent, under wings and abdomen. You will need to re-apply in seven to ten days. It would be wise to dust all your birds at this time.

Q: Help! I have two teenage roosters and they are constantly fighting.

All chickens will 'spar' with their siblings and others to establish their place in the pecking order. It's natural for cockerels to run at each other, bump chests and try to stare down the opponent. Whoever backs off first is the loser. As long as they aren't drawing blood or hurting each other let them be.

Q: A friend told me to give my birds vinegar to drink, should I?

Your friend is probably talking about natural apple cider vinegar. A tablespoon per gallon of water is said to help chickens fight off disease especially respiratory problems. I give it to them in Fall and Winter two to three times a week.

Tip: Do not put it into metal containers as it will react with the metal.

Q: My pullet laid a blood covered egg this morning, what should I do?

This is a fairly common occurrence in new layers. Check out her rear end to make sure she isn't still bleeding, if she is wipe away the blood and keep her separate until it stops, otherwise her sisters may make matters worse.

Printed in Great Britain
by Amazon